AF781728

ECONOMIC ISSUES, PROBLEMS AND PERSPECTIVES

SELF-REGULATION OF MARKET ECONOMY

INTERDISCIPLINARY ANALYSIS

ECONOMIC ISSUES, PROBLEMS AND PERSPECTIVES

Additional books in this series can be found on Nova's website under the Series tab.

Additional e-books in this series can be found on Nova's website under the e-book tab.

ECONOMIC ISSUES, PROBLEMS AND PERSPECTIVES

SELF-REGULATION OF MARKET ECONOMY

INTERDISCIPLINARY ANALYSIS

PAATA LEIASHVILY

nova publishers
New York

Copyright © 2015 by Nova Science Publishers, Inc.

All rights reserved. No part of this book may be reproduced, stored in a retrieval system or transmitted in any form or by any means: electronic, electrostatic, magnetic, tape, mechanical photocopying, recording or otherwise without the written permission of the Publisher.

We have partnered with Copyright Clearance Center to make it easy for you to obtain permissions to reuse content from this publication. Simply navigate to this publication's page on Nova's website and locate the "Get Permission" button below the title description. This button is linked directly to the title's permission page on copyright.com. Alternatively, you can visit copyright.com and search by title, ISBN, or ISSN.

For further questions about using the service on copyright.com, please contact:
Copyright Clearance Center
Phone: +1-(978) 750-8400 Fax: +1-(978) 750-4470 E-mail: info@copyright.com.

NOTICE TO THE READER

The Publisher has taken reasonable care in the preparation of this book, but makes no expressed or implied warranty of any kind and assumes no responsibility for any errors or omissions. No liability is assumed for incidental or consequential damages in connection with or arising out of information contained in this book. The Publisher shall not be liable for any special, consequential, or exemplary damages resulting, in whole or in part, from the readers' use of, or reliance upon, this material. Any parts of this book based on government reports are so indicated and copyright is claimed for those parts to the extent applicable to compilations of such works.

Independent verification should be sought for any data, advice or recommendations contained in this book. In addition, no responsibility is assumed by the publisher for any injury and/or damage to persons or property arising from any methods, products, instructions, ideas or otherwise contained in this publication.

This publication is designed to provide accurate and authoritative information with regard to the subject matter covered herein. It is sold with the clear understanding that the Publisher is not engaged in rendering legal or any other professional services. If legal or any other expert assistance is required, the services of a competent person should be sought. FROM A DECLARATION OF PARTICIPANTS JOINTLY ADOPTED BY A COMMITTEE OF THE AMERICAN BAR ASSOCIATION AND A COMMITTEE OF PUBLISHERS.

Additional color graphics may be available in the e-book version of this book.

Library of Congress Cataloging-in-Publication Data

ISBN: 978-1-63483-324-0

Published by Nova Science Publishers, Inc. † New York

CONTENTS

Preface		**vii**
Acknowledgment		**xi**
Abstract		**xiii**
Introduction		**xv**
Chapter 1	Interdisciplinary Discourse	**1**
Chapter 2	Dialectics of Economic Categories	**11**
Chapter 3	"Symmetric Model" of Economic Equilibrium	**31**
Chapter 4	Operational Closeness of Complex Systems	**63**
Chapter 5	Business Cycles	**73**
Chapter 6	Enigma of Adam Smith	**89**
Conclusion		**101**
References		**116**
Index		**119**

PREFACE

Due to the dialectical analysis of the fundamental economic categories, market economy appears as a complex, nonlinear, operationally closed (but causally open) system of economic actions. Such systems have a number of unique properties that have been well studied in chaos theory, constructivism and second-order cybernetics. This enables of the study of economic processes to attract unique research and developments of these sciences within the format of interdisciplinary analysis. In this regard, many ideas from "meta theories" of sociologists are of particular importance; Talcott Parsons, relative to the system of social actions, and Niklas Luhmann, regarding the operational closeness and causal openness, self-reference and autopoiesis of social systems, etc. On the basis of interdisciplinary analysis of decentralized economic system we get an entirely new interpretation of economic categories and relations between them; we obtain a new understanding of economic equilibrium, cyclical fluctuations and the processes of economic reproduction.

The main contradiction that drives the economic system is that each subject consumes something that others produce and produces what others consume. Therefore, one wants to buy something that belongs to another person and sells something that other people lack, but belongs to him. That is, the satisfaction of one's own needs is mediated by the satisfaction of others' needs. Thanks to this, all subjects are attached to each other by their action, forming a single whole, a system in which all that is produced is consumed and all that is consumed - is produced. In such conditions, each economic action generates another action. That is, there arise recursive processes, owing to which the economic system becomes closed self-reproducible system generating its own elements.

For an adequate understanding of reproduction process of economy as a complex self-organizing system, one must clearly understand the difference between the "causal openness" and "operational closeness" of the system. Under the causal openness the principle is implied which is underlying in the basis of interchange of matter and energy of economic system with its environment, be it the physical nature, human body or other social subsystems. In addition, under the operational or organizational closeness the principle is meant, which forms the inherent structure of the economic system providing self-organization processes of decentralized economy. Based on our concept, we suggest a model, which will reflect the organizational closeness of economic system and thereby identify the mechanisms to ensure the autonomy of its functioning.

Organizational closeness of a system is caused by interconnection of all economic functions (production, consumption, demand, supply, investment, etc.), which form a closed structure in a single system. This makes it possible to understand the reproductive process as a circular process in which results of economic activity become its own premises. That is, an economic system appears as autopoietic system that creates elements, which it is composed of. In result of this approach, we find that the self-organization of a market economy is carried out thanks to a recursive processes (commodities are produced by commodities, prices are formed on the basis of prices, actions generate actions, satisfied needs create new unsatisfied needs, etc.). Recursive processes in the economic system as well as in other complex nonlinear dynamical systems generate "eigenvalues" ("fixed points" - in the terminology of mathematics). The equilibrium prices are just such "eigenvalues" to which the actual market prices strive because of recursive processes ensuring the movement of system to the general equilibrium.

Since the market economy at one and the same time is a operationally closed and causally open system, it tends to equilibrium within the system (between the intra-systemic processes) and is in a non-equilibrium state regarding the environment. Internal equilibrium and stability are necessary to preserve the integrity of a system, but non-equilibrium and instability regarding the environment is a necessary condition for the development of system. Therefore, the economic system is able to homeostasis and thus is able to develop, change the states, react to external influences and adapt to the environment. Therefore, it will be capable to establish a dynamic equilibrium.

In the monograph a mathematical model of general economic equilibrium is proposed, i.e. the model of the attractor - a relatively stable, latent structure of that state of the economic system, towards which the decentralized economy always strives by virtue of the immanent logic of the development of intra-system processes (but never reaches it due to the permanent impact of random external factors – changes in natural and social environment). Mathematical models of nonlinear complex systems show that such systems "hide" a certain form of organization of intra-processes that are caused solely by their own non-linear properties. That is, structure-attractors can be interpreted as teleological structures, which determine the main trends in the system's evolution.

The dialectical analysis of the essence of economic phenomena and a model developed on its basis reveal the hidden relationships between gross profit and gross saving, gross investment and gross consumption in debt and many other relationships between economic parameters, which cannot be detected by other methods of research. Although neoclassical theory fixes the relationship between saving and investment, nevertheless, it is not aware of the interdependence between saving and profits, also between investment and consumption in debt as well. So it is not aware of the links between all the above-mentioned categories (i.e. saving, profits, investment and consumption in debt), which exist within a closed economic system. But without this, it is impossible to understand how the reproduction is performed, how the general equilibrium is formed, how business cycles occur. Therefore, without understanding of these processes it is not possible to create an adequate mathematical model of a decentralized economic system and develop an effective economic policy.

ACKNOWLEDGMENT

The goals of this study are identification of self-regulating and self-reproducing mechanisms of a market economy. In result of the dialectical study of essence of economy it appears as a operationally closed complex nonlinear system. Like other such systems, it has a number of unique properties that are studied by chaos theory, constructivism, and second-order cybernetics. Study of these properties allows us to give answers to many questions of economic theory, to create effective mathematical models and work out an adequate economic policy.

It is assumed within the study: on the basis of the theory of social action to present economic system as a system of economic actions; based on the dialectical analysis of the fundamental economic categories to present the market economy as a operationally closed complex system of economic actions; develop the mathematical model of operationally closed and causally open decentralized economic system; identify an economic mechanism of self-organization and self-reproduction on the basis of analysis of recursive processes; reveal the essence of general economic equilibrium and homeostasis mechanisms of economic system based on the ideas of constructivism and second order cybernetics; discover the mechanisms of formation of business cycles based on chaos theory concepts.

ABSTRACT

In this monograph Prof. P. Leiashvily, in result of dialectical analysis of economic processes, presents the market economy as a complex, non-linear, operationally closed, and causally open system. Such systems have a number of unique properties that have been well studied in chaos theory, constructivism and second-order cybernetics. Based on an interdisciplinary analysis of market economy, in the discourse of constructivism and second-order cybernetics, a fundamentally new approach is given to the analysis of general economic equilibrium and business cycles. *On the basis of the obtained results, the analysis of reproduction process is done.* The monograph offers "Symmetric model" of general equilibrium. This is a model of economic system in which the self-organization is performed thanks to a recursive processes. Based on the analysis of a simple economic reproduction, significant shortcomings of existing calculating methods of the basic macroeconomic indicators of the System of National Accounts (GDP, GNI and others) are shown. Methodological basis for their adequate calculation is given.

Keywords: Dialectics, constructivism, second-order cybernetics, chaos theory, economic equilibrium, business cycles, simple reproduction, recursive processes, complex non-linear system, operational closeness, macroeconomic indicators

Prof. Paata Leiashvily
Professor of Tbilisi State University,
Department of Economics
Address: St. Kandelaki, 2. Apt. 22.
Tbilisi, Georgia, 0160, e-mail: palepano@gmail.com.

INTRODUCTION

It has long been realized that the neoclassical theory does not adequately reflect the reality. But the global crisis of 2008 has finally convinced many economists that economics itself is in the deep crisis. The modern economy is unable to function normally without the government regulation, without development of effective economic policy. This requires the clear understanding of essence of economic processes, the necessary theoretical knowledge. But the recent worldwide crisis has shown the economic science still lacks sufficient knowledge for creation of the adequate models, correct prediction of economic processes and development of effective policy recommendations. Moreover, economic policy, based on a false understanding of processes, itself contributes to above-mentioned crisis. Just as Keynes (with J. Robinson, P. Sraffa, and others) has laid the intellectual responsibility for the crisis of 1929 on the marginalist theory, today the responsibility for the crisis in 2008 should be put on the neoclassical theory. At the same time it becomes increasingly clear that not only certain thesis, but the very mainstream needs a fundamental rethinking. Economic science is facing a serious challenge. Respectively, more and more economists around the world are convinced of this.

Economic knowledge is acquired through cognition of economic reality. This knowledge has an influence on economic policy, education, worldview of politicians, experts and economic subjects. All this stipulates economic decisions and actions of the subjects. But totality of these actions just forms that economic reality, which is studied by economics. Therefore, collective actions depend on the knowledge and knowledge depends on collective actions. That is, a circular causality arises - the object of knowledge depends on the results of knowledge. Since neoclassical theory is unaware of this circular causality, in this theory it takes the form of a logical "vicious circle." Thus, it cannot provide an adequate economic theory and develop effective policies.

The above-mentioned "vicious circle" is caused by the false methodology of neoclassical theory. According to this methodology the neoclassical theory studies only economic phenomena, that is, the surface of economic reality, but does not study the essence of these phenomena, because it does not recognize its existence and does not own the methods of its investigation. But what happens in the economic reality at the level of empirical facts, to a large extent, is caused by it itself.

But only the processes occurring at the empirical level, that is something which is studied by neoclassical theory, depend on the actions of economic agents. The essence of a market economy does not depend on these actions. On the contrary, they themselves are caused by this essence. Therefore, it is necessary to examine the essence of economic processes. But to explore the essence is possible only by dialectical method of research that significantly differs from the methods of neoclassical research.

In result of investigation of the essence, the market economy appears as a operationally closed complex nonlinear system. Like all such systems, it has a number of unique properties, which are studied by second-order cybernetics, constructivism and chaos theory. The study of these properties allows us to give answers to many questions, to create effective mathematical models and to develop adequate economic policy.

After the beginning of the 50s, when K. Arrow, G. Debreu and, independently of them L. McKenzie, have published their models of general equilibrium, the mathematical direction of economics has received a new stimulus of development. By the intellectual efforts of these authors the base of modern mathematical models of closed decentralized economic system has been laid. For last several decades vast stream of works have been devoted to the theory of general equilibrium. Some scientists consider the results received in this area of science to be one of the meaningful achievements of mathematical branch of economic theory in the second half of XX century. But in their attempts to create adequate model of general equilibrium, economists have so much been concentrated on purely mathematical side of the problem that unintentionally have followed a way, which leads "nowhere" (Kaldor). Even M. Morishima, who has devoted all his life to research of the general equilibrium and has largely contributed to development of this direction of the theory, writes: "It is also the case that the world of GET is in fact a dream world, the world which is not totally workable in the context of actual society," (Morishima, 1991, p.71).

In result of global economic crisis 2008 - 2010 all current models of economic equilibrium, including the AGE, CGE and DSGE models, have been discredited.[1] Moreover, this crisis has detected not only incompetence of existing models of equilibrium, but also the serious problems in the very paradigm of economic theory, which forms a basis for construction of these models. This circumstance pushes on the thought that failures in creation of adequate models are caused not by an insufficient readiness of actually mathematical toolkit, but by the incorrect assumptions on which they are constructed.

In spite of the fact that more than century efforts (since Walras) of theorist economists to create an adequate mathematical model of closed decentralized economic system have not been yet crowned with desirable results, the idea of general equilibrium is so attractive that economists will not yet refuse it in the nearest future. With the acknowledgement of this premise, another attempt is in this investigation to clarify the understanding of regularities for both formation of general equilibrium and deviations from it, which are evident in business cycle fluctuations.

The idea of economic equilibrium is closely related to the idea of economic reproduction or the problem of *circular flow*, as it is called in neoclassical tradition. This is one of the most important problems of economics that needs rethinking. Since the publication of "Economic Table" by F. Quesnay (1758), within the 250-year history of evolution of circular flow theory, the scholars such as A. Smith, D. Ricardo, K. Marx, W. Bortkiewicz, J. Schumpeter, V. Leontief, P. Sraffa, P. Samuelson, M. Morishima and others have concentrated much attention on this problem. And although the term "circular flow" figures among the concepts of mainstream, it has gradually lost its sense of scientific research program. It remains only a means to illustrate the "model of circular flows" expounded in the textbooks in chapter on the national accounting. The impression exists that the problem of circular flow (reproduction), like a problem of value with which it is closely related, finds no satisfactory solution and is gradually pushed to the periphery of scientific interests and is gradually "forgotten" by neoclassicists. But these are the

[1] "The point I am making is that the DSGE model has nothing useful to say about antirecession policy because it has built into its essentially implausible assumptions the "conclusion" that there is nothing for macroeconomic policy to do. I think we have just seen how untrue this is for an economy attached to a highly-leveraged, weakly-regulated financial system" (Solow, 2010).

fundamental problems of economic theory, without solution of which, economics cannot overcome the deplorable state in which it is today. However, apart from the purely theoretical significance, the problem of circular flow has practical importance and is associated with the construction of foundations of national accounting. Accordingly, the lack of a clear understanding of reproductive process causes serious deficiencies in the System of National Accounts.

In the present work, based on the results of dialectical analysis of some fundamental economic categories and on the main ideas of Walras equilibrium theory, a "symmetric model" of general equilibrium is proposed and on its basis a new interpretation of reproduction process is given. Based on new understanding of reproduction process, the attempt is made to solve the so-called "Enigma of Smith," which will be discussed below, and which allows to reveal the theoretical failure of calculation methods of macroeconomic indicators GDP and GNI.

Chapter 1

INTERDISCIPLINARY DISCOURSE

1. To exit from the crisis economics must take greater account of the achievements of other sciences and implement interdisciplinary research. In this regard, scientific ideas arising within constructivism deserve special attention. As an independent branch of the philosophy of science, constructivism emerges in the 80s and soon attracts the attention of scientists. Constructivism is gradually gaining more and more influence in contemporary epistemology.[2] However, the problems of constructivism go far beyond epistemology. It is amazing but constructivism is built into the inner core of cybernetic theoretical concepts. Cybernetics creates constructivism as its logical continuation. From the very beginning of its existence, from the 1940-1950s (the concept of N. Wiener, U. Ross Ashby, X. von Foerster), one of its central concepts is the idea of circular causality. This idea is central to the theoretical constructions of constructivism.

2. A good example of circular causality can serve the aforementioned dependence of cognition of economic reality on the results of this cognition. On the basis of his knowledge the actor interacts with reality, adapts to it, and adapts the reality to himself. Actor and reality do change each other during the interaction. After all, as a result of observing, the actor receives the knowledge about reality. And it is clear that the actions of the actor cannot be the same before and after the acquisition of new knowledge about the existing reality because along with their change the nature of these actions also changes. And

---

[2] Constructivist paradigm emerged based on research results of a number of related disciplines, at the junction of natural sciences and humanities. In its formation a great role is played by the scientific ideas of psychologist J. Piaget, biologists and neuroscientists U. Maturana and F. Varela, cybernetics and philosopher H.fon Foerster, engineer and mathematician J. Spencer-Brown, epistemologist, anthropologist and ecologist G. Beytson and others.

it is clear that the results of observations, i.e. the knowledge, cannot remain unchanged before and after the interaction acts with reality, because the observable reality changes as a result of these interaction acts. Here is a circular causality.

Here, the effect caused by some reason, itself becomes the reason causing the effect. Action generates the action, the cause generates the cause and they both generate each other. Cause and effect are merged into one. This is an activity that has become the cause of itself, or self-generation activities. Formally, this process can be expressed in general form as: $x = F(x)$, where x - is the interaction between any elements of a system, and F - is the form of the relationship between these processes. Systems, in which such circular processes are carried out, are called self-referential systems, which are studied by second-order cybernetics and constructivism. Such systems are autonomous, operationally closed and have unique properties.

An interesting feature of these systems is that they have so-called "Eigen-Values," "Eigen-Functions," "Eigen-Algorithms," "Eigen-Behaviors." The fact is that in the processes of interaction with the environment there is no unequivocal correspondence between input and output. The reaction of such a system to the impacts of environment depends not only on the nature of this impact, but also on the state of system, which in turn is caused by the previous state and previous impacts of environment. And the output reaction affects its subsequent change. The system evolves and gets its history. In other words, the output is not a direct response to the input stimulus. It depends on the intrinsic structure of the system, its current state and those recursive processes that have been initiated by the input signal. Such behavior of system assumes the character of "Eigen-Behaviors" and it cannot be considered to be a simple response to external stimuli in the direct sense of the word.

Constructivism has a strong influence on sociology. German scholar Niklas Luhmann (1927-1998) is one of the first who has built a system of social philosophy on the fundamental ideas of constructivism, such as the ideas of theory of complex self-organizing systems, autopoiesis, operational closure and causal openness, self-reference, structural coupling, contingency, etc. Proceedings of N. Luhmann represent a sociological version of constructivism and are mentioned already as classic works on a par with the works of E. Glasersfeld, H. von Foerster, W. Maturana, F. Varela, and other famous constructionists. In contrast to sociologists, due to the dogmatism prevailing in modern economics, economists have shown indifference toward new ideas of the constructivists.

3. As a result of dialectical analysis of economic phenomena and processes, the market economy appears as a operationally closed complex system, which has all the properties that are well studied in the second-order cybernetics and about which constructivists write. Out of the separate actions of million independent economic subjects, who act in their own selfish interests, depending on the actions performed by these functions, the various economic flows are formed. These flows in the scale of society form the functional structure of a closed complex nonlinear system - a market economy. The market economy is a complex self-organized autopoiesis system, the primary element of which is economic action.

The structural functional analysis of this system leads to a fundamentally new understanding of how the self-regulation of decentralized economy occurs, how the economic cycles arise. This method of analysis has long been successfully used in sociology but, unfortunately, in economic theory proper attention is not given to it. Thanks to the work of sociologists Talcott Parsons and Robert Merton, structural functionalism reached the greatest influence in the 1950-1960s, but in the second half of the 1960s more and more intensified criticism of this approach appeared from different perspectives. After a long decline of interest in the theory of Parsons, from the 80s the interest in functionalism has renewed. The most prominent representatives of "neo-functionalism" are sociologists N. Luhmann, J. Alexander and R. Munch. The role of N. Luhmann should be especially emphasized, whose name is associated with fundamental rethinking of basic concepts of functionalism of the latest advances in the theory of complex systems and methodology of constructivism.

Scientific concepts of sociologists, attempting to explain social phenomena from the perspective of the theory of complex systems, are developed in detail, have a long history and intensive research in this direction continues. Similar attempts to explore the society within the context of the theory of complex systems are undertaken in the framework of synergetics as a scientific paradigm. However, the difference between these two approaches is that in its methodology synergetics is based on the positivism, but constructivists are more inclined to transcendental phenomenology and thus fully take into account the specifics of society not only as a living system, but also as a cogitative, policontextual, semantic system.[3]

[3] There is a close connection between constructivism and synergetics. Like synergetics, constructivism is the result of a generalization of a number of scientific concepts and researches in various areas of knowledge. It is interesting that many of these concepts belong to both discourses. Therefore, along with the names of the founders of synergetics -

Structural functionalism sees society or other social objects as a system, as a structurally dissected integrity, in which each system unit performs a specific function, creating conditions for the normal functioning of all subsystems and of the system as a whole. The main problem that sociologists try to explain on the basis of functionalism is - How is the social order under conditions of free activity of individuals, pursuing their own interests? How does a social mechanism operate that leads to mutual coordination of their actions in the public interest? As we see, sociologists of this direction see for themselves the basic scientific problem like economists, beginning from Adam Smith, have seen in relation to the decentralized economic system. Economic theory can discover for itself many valuable ideas in very interesting scientific developments of sociologists.

The functioning of society is the cumulative result of interactions of an infinite set of individuals. To understand the society as a system, it is necessary, in this chaos of interactions and absolute social mobility of subjects in the social space and time, to reveal something relatively sustained and stable, i.e. structure. In the structural-functional paradigm the structure of a system of social actions is understood as a set of relatively stable relationships between the elements thanks to which the system maintains its integrity and functionality in a transformation process under influence of external or internal factors. There is no structure outside the system and there is no system without the structure. They imply each other. Concrete individuals are born and die, begin and end socially active life, replace each other, but the social structures remain. That is, structures are not strictly tied to the actions of certain individuals. Accordingly, social systems are not composed of people. These are the people, who are involved in them, and by performing certain functions by their actions support their existence.

I. Prigogine, H. Haken, E. Lorentz, B. Mandelbrot, etc., more often the names of H. von Foerster, U. Maturana, F. Varela and others are mentioned, who laid the foundations of constructivism. However, between synergetics and constructivism differences also exist. Although in general, they have a common methodological and philosophical installation, in constructivism relatively more attention is paid to the epistemology and functioning of living systems, but in the spotlight of synergetics the ontological context of studies is, while the processes of learning and life are considered only as applied aspects of the functioning of non-equilibrium systems. In synergetics it comes about open non-equilibrium systems in general, but radical constructivism focuses on the process of maintaining homeostasis in living cognitive systems. In the conception of constructivism the self-organization of complex systems is based on the principle of feedback, which gives them stability. In synergetics this principle is of secondary importance, since the focus is on the dynamics of the system, balancing on the verge of chaos and order.

4. In this concept, we adhere to the standpoint of Talcott Parsons, according to which the constitutive element of society, as a social system, is social action, and society is a system of social actions.[4] At that, the economy is a kind of social system and economic action – a kind of social action. The term "social action" T. Parsons borrowed from sociological theory of Max Weber, according to which social action is a unit of social reality, its primary constituent element. Social action is an *action* because for actors it has subjective meaning, and is *social* because according to this sense it relates to the actions of others and is focused on them (See: Weber, 1990). Through their actions all subjects are interconnected into a single system. Each action of the subject affects the actions of other subjects and the system as a whole. Each action has another action as a reaction. The action is a function of the expected reaction and the reaction is a function of action, which causes it.

If we consider, for example, only economic subsystem, all actors, whether individuals, businesses, organizations, households, churches, universities, government agencies, etc. - all of them, in one way or another, participate in the economic process, perform in it a particular function. But none of these subjects is purely economic subject and in one way or another each of them is involved in the functioning of other, non-economic subsystems. That is, all subjects are multifunctional. So naturally, unit or indivisible part of economical subsystem cannot be a holistic subject that performs not only economic roles, but who is also an actor of other subsystems of society. Economic subsystem does not cover all the actions of concrete subjects, whether individuals or groups, but their actions only in the specific role perform economic functions. The element of economic subsystem may be only those actions of subject, which perform some or other economic functions, i.e. only economic action. Therefore, as a subsystem of society, the economy is a system of economic *actions,* but not a system consisting of *subjects.* Weber defines economics as "autocephalous system of economic action."

5. An elementary action "… is the "smallest" unit of an action system, which still makes sense as a part of a concrete system of action" (Parsons, 1949, 731). Elementary action (unit act) is the ultimate unity only in a system of actions, but by itself it does not constitute an indecomposable entity. It itself

[4] K. Marx believed that society was a set of social relations; T. Parsons believed that it was a system of social actions; N. Luhmann believed that it was a system of communication. But, anyway, despite the various arguments, along with many other social scientists, they agree that the primary element of society (in the special sociological sense) is not an individual. Individuals form a society with their relationships, actions or communications, but they are not directly the primary elements with which society is constituted.

is composed of components, such as the end, conditions, means of one or more norms governing the choice of means to achieve the end (See ibid.). To describe the actions requires an appropriate frame of reference, which is essentially a framework of relations between the elements of action. Without such a framework to talk about the action does not make sense. "... the schema is inherently subjective ... . This is most clearly indicated by the fact that the normative elements can be conceived as "existing" only in the mind of the actor. They can become accessible to an observer in any other form only through realization, which precludes any analysis of their causal relation to action" (Ibid, 733). T. Parsons writes:

> "Every physical phenomenon must involve processes in time, which happen to particles which can be located in space. It is impossible to talk about physical processes in any other terms, at least so long as the conceptual scheme of the classical physics is employed. Similarly, it is impossible even to talk about action in terms that do not involve a means-end relationship with all the implications just discussed. ... Thus the action frame of reference may be said to have what many, following Husserl, have called a "phenomenological" status. ... It is not a phenomenon in the empirical sense. It is the indispensable logical framework in which we describe and think about the phenomena of action" (Ibid, 733).

As we see it is important to distinguish between the actions themselves and empirical processes. In this context remark by Ludwig von Mises is also interesting:

> "Economics is not about things and tangible material objects; it is about men, their meanings and actions. Goods, commodities, and wealth and all the other notions of conduct are not elements of nature; they are elements of human meaning and conduct. He who wants to deal with them must not look at the external world; he must search for them in the meaning of acting men" (Mises, 1996, p.92) Also: "Production is not something physical, material, and external; it is a spiritual and intellectual phenomenon" (Ibid, p.141).

6. According to the structural-functional approach the economy appears as a system of economic actions. But, according to the said above, the economic action is not purely empirical process. Economic actions are such only because of the meanings and values, which a man gives them. Therefore, the economy as a system of economic actions exists only in human consciousness and is a

system of senses and values. The empirical processes that correspond to the economic actions in the real world by themselves are not economic actions, but only the causal processes that take place according to the laws of nature.

After all, the facts themselves are not *economic* facts. All depends on the ends and needs, which have provoked them, on the relation of the subject to the existing and the due. Consequently, the subjects perceive in different ways one and the same objective facts. For example, production or consumption, as such, does not exist objectively. Only the transformations of some objects into others, according to the laws of nature, exist objectively. But whether or not a man would call it production or consumption - depends on his attitude to this process. Accordingly, he will be called producer or consumer. Also, whether or not he perceives these or other objects as products or resources, and whether or not he perceives them as the embodiment of costs or utilities, depends on this, etc. The same with all other economic categories - they are relative and exist only in human consciousness.

Although a person by his economic actions provokes some empirical processes, these processes exist as the real facts. But his attitude to these processes, which causes this or that perception of the facts, exists only in his consciousness and constantly changes together with his needs and ends. That is why, the same fact is perceived differently by different persons and even by the same person, depending on his needs and the ends. One and the same object or process performs different functions at the same time, simultaneously exists in different relations to different subjects and objects, therefore, simultaneously is, for example, product, and resource, or buying and selling, import and export, credit and debt, and so on. In this (and only in this) sense, we can say that economic processes exist only in human consciousness. Economy is just his attitude to these processes through the prism of his needs, his understanding of due. And here is no mysticism in this. To be a producer, consumer, product, resource, etc. - all this is not inseparable real properties of objects or subjects, but the functions that they perform. It is impossible to produce a product, not being a consumer of resources. Therefore, he also is a consumer. But he is not only producer and consumer. He is also the seller and the buyer, investor and saver, creditor and debtor, etc. And in conditions of division of labor, each of these functions he can perform each of these functions only as one party, in collaboration with other economic actors. So, in a market economy, he can be producer only because someone else is a consumer; can be a seller - because someone else is buyer; lender - because someone else is debtor, etc. (See: Leiashvily, 2013).

By its result every action in some way excites the need for response to it. For the result of every action is a means for the other actions, the product is a resource for other actions. The product of each action creates the need, according to which it itself becomes a resource, i.e. creates the need for another action in which this product itself will be consumed. Moreover, if the product cannot be transformed into a resource, it will not be considered as a product. From the very beginning the product is produced as a resource for future action. Therefore, each action in itself already implies the need for another action. And if it cannot find its continuation, it itself will appear invalid, fictitious (See: Leiashvily, 2012; 2011).

7. Actions differ from each other by their function. The function can exist in reality only being implemented and, therefore, only with the action. In reality, the function does not exist separately from the action, which it performs, as well as the action cannot exist without performing this or that function. There is no action without the particular function; if the action belongs to the system, it performs defined function. Therefore, each economic action not only creates other action like itself, but creates "its other" action. This "its other" action, being the same economic action, is identical with it. Otherwise it will not belong to this system, but it will be something belonging to the environment. And at the same time, "its other" action differs from its parent action by its function. It performs the function conjugate with it, which necessarily is implied by a function of parent action.

As we have already noted, in a market economy, the action, having a function of producing some product (using the consumption of some other goods) means "its other" action, which has the function of consumption of produced good. But since the action for production of good and "its other" action for consumption of this good is performed by different actors, the produced good before being consumed must be sold by producer, and bought by consumer; and thus must be supplied to the market by producer; hence, the consumer should demand this product before he buys and consumes it; then he must supply money for sale or other good; therefore, he acts not only as consumer, but also as producer, which also must give rise to a similar sequence of economic actions, as well as producer of goods he consumes, etc. That is, a sequence of actions appears, the functions of which are interrelated. The circular organization of interrelated functions is formed.

Moreover, each of the economic actors simultaneously is a producer and consumer, seller and buyer, investor and consumer in debt, entrepreneur and saver, creditor and debtor. It is impossible to be a producer of goods, not being a consumer of other goods and it is impossible to be a consumer, not being a producer, and it is impossible to be either one or the other, without being the seller of the goods and the buyer of other goods, and it is impossible to be either the seller or the buyer of the goods not being a buyer and seller of money.

8. In the end, we find that all the functions performed by different actors are also interrelated as the actions, which perform these functions. All of them generate each other. Each action creates "its other" action and itself is generated by others, because itself is "its other for its other." Through this they reproduce the structure of system. A functionally closed structure of a system or operational closeness, that is a circular organization of intersystem functions, is reproduced by the sequence of performed actions; for reproduction of this sequence of actions is caused just by the very functions, which are performed by each of these actions. The sequence of actions causes the reproduction of circular organization of functions. Their circular organization determines this sequence of actions, thanks to which each action generates "its other" action, and it is just that other action, being a necessary link in the sequence, which reproduces the circular organization of functions.

In this functional closeness of structure the essence of economic subsystem of society, based on a division of labor, is just reflected; these functions only show the relationships between themselves. They are closely interrelated and refer to each other as positive and negative: consumption and production, selling and buying, supply and demand, investment and consumption in debt, credit and debt, making profits and making saving, entrepreneurship function and saving function, etc. Opposites can come into clash only because they are in relation and form a unit, in which one moment is needed as well as another. These functions cannot exist without each other. They make a single whole, closed structure, where everything is relative, where all relate to each other as positive and negative, where one cannot exist without the other. The "symmetric model," considered below, which reflects the functional closeness of economic system, reflects the *essential relationship* of a market economy and, thus, reflects in itself the *essence* of economic system in which everything is relative and all are in reflective relationships to one other.[5]

[5] "In the sphere of Essence one category does not pass into another, but refers to another merely. In Being, the form of reference is purely due to our reflection on what takes place: but it is the special and proper characteristic of Essence. In the sphere of Being, when somewhat becomes another, the somewhat has vanished. Not so in Essence: here there is no real other, but only diversity, reference of the one to its other. The transition of Essence is therefore at the same time no transition: for in the passage of different into different, the different does not vanish: the different terms remain in their relation. When we speak of Being and

It follows from the foregoing that for the analysis of market economy in the constructivist discourse, it should be presented in the form of a operationally or organizationally closed complex system. But to identify this operational or organizational closeness, first must be identified the dialectical relationships between the fundamental economic categories, which cannot be detected by traditional methods of neoclassical theory. Dialectical analysis of these categories as a necessary precondition for building a "symmetric model" of operationally closed decentralized economic system is given below.

Nought, Being is independent, so is Nought. The case is otherwise with the Positive and the Negative. No doubt these possess the characteristic of Being and Nought. But the Positive by itself has no sense; it is wholly in reference to the negative. And it is the same with the negative. In the sphere of Being the reference of one term to another is only implicit; in Essence, on the contrary, it is explicit. And this in general is the distinction between the forms of Being and Essence: in Being everything is immediate, in Essence everything is relative" (Hegel, 1974, 262-263.)

Chapter 2

DIALECTICS OF ECONOMIC CATEGORIES

1. SURPLUS PRODUCT AND SURPLUS RESOURCE

1. To identify the organizational closeness of market economy you must first reveal the deep inner connection, which exists between production and consumption in general, and between production and consumption sectors of economy - in particular. Production and consumption are the opposites, inextricably linked with each other, are the unity of opposites. The process of production itself is a process of resource consumption, and consumption of recourses is production of goods. Brilliant analysis of this dialectic, Marx gives in "Outline of the Critique of Political Economy (*Grundrisse*)":

> "Production, then, is also immediately consumption, consumption is also immediately production. Each is immediately its opposite" (Маркс, 1958, 717). "The identities between consumption and production thus appear threefold: (1) *Immediate identity:* Production is consumption, consumption is production. Consumptive production. Productive consumption. The political economists call both productive consumption, ... (2) [In the sense] that one appears as a means for the other, is mediated by the other: this is expressed as their mutual dependence; a movement which relates them to one another, makes them appear indispensable to one another, but still leaves them external to each other. Production creates the material, as external object, for consumption; consumption creates the need, as internal object, as aim, for production. Without production no consumption; without consumption no production. ... (3) Not only is production immediately consumption and consumption immediately production, not only is production a means for consumption and consumption the aim of production, i.e. each supplies the other with

> its object (production supplying the external object of consumption, consumption the conceived object of production); but also, each of them, apart from being immediately the other, and apart from mediating the other, in addition to this creates the other in completing itself, and creates itself as the other. ... Thereupon, nothing simpler for a Hegelian than to posit production and consumption as identical (Ibid, 719 -720).

So, it's not two different processes, but one and the same process, seen from different points of view. In fact, they are two different aspects of the same process of converting resources into products. In a market economy, where products and resources take the form of commodities, this process takes the form of transformation of some commodities into others or, if expressed in the sense of P. Sraffa, "the production of commodities by means of consumption of commodities." Due to this circumstance the production sector and consumption sector are also inseparably linked, but although they are "in the external relation to each other," each of them by itself is a unity of production and consumption. In this sense, they are identical. But since each of them consumes what the other produces, then in this sense, they are also opposed. They are identical and opposite simultaneously and form a dialectical contradiction, just that which drives the economy.

2. The matter is that for production entrepreneurs buy from owners not the production factors (Labor, Land, Capital), but only the rights of temporary use of services of these production factors. Payments for them are wage, interest and rent. And entrepreneurs sell to them (and to each other) entrepreneurial services and make a profit. Primary economic resources for entrepreneurs are just the right of temporary use of the services of production factors, which they buy from their owners. But if this is so, regardless of whether production factors themselves are reproducible or irreproducible, in all cases, the primary resources *as commodities* are *reproducible goods*. Reproduction of primary resources as commodities is reduced to reproduction of life of owners of production factors, only which have the right to sell these "rights of use." For the reproduction of property rights for production factors and their services, reproduction of subjects of these rights is reduced. They sell the services of production factors and keep them (production factors) as a permanent source of incomes just because they do not sell the production factors themselves. Thus, the approach of Marx to the question of buying the right to use the labor force in the market economy should be extended to other production factors. With respect to the owners of the labor force, he writes:

"The exchange of commodities of itself implies no other relations of dependence than those which, result from its own nature. On this assumption, labour-power can appear upon the market as a commodity, only if, and so far as, its possessor, the individual whose labour-power it is, offers it for sale, or sells it, as a commodity. In order that he may be able to do this, he must have it at his disposal, must be the untrammelled owner of his capacity for labour, i.e., of his person. He and the owner of money meet in the market, and deal with each other as on the basis of equal rights, with this difference alone, that one is buyer, the other seller; both, therefore, equal in the eyes of the law. The continuance of this relation demands that the owner of the labour-power should sell it only for a definite period, for if he were to sell it rump and stump, once for all, he would be selling himself, converting himself from a free man into a slave, from an owner of a commodity into a commodity. He must constantly look upon his labour-power as his own property, his own commodity, and this he can only do by placing it at the disposal of the buyer temporarily, for a definite period of time. By this means alone can he avoid renouncing his rights of ownership over it" (M, 1978, 178). "Therefore the labour-time requisite for the production of labour-power reduces itself to that necessary for the production of those means of subsistence; in other words, the value of labour-power is the value of the means of subsistence necessary for the maintenance of the labourer" (Ibid, 181).

The difference in reproduction of owners of labor force and of other production factors is only that in case of reproduction of owner of labor force, a labor force, as the ability to work, is reproduced too. For it is the ability of the owner. But in case of owner of other production factors, reproduction of owner does not mean the physical reproduction of the Capital or of the Earth. In this case, the property exists separately from the owner. Therefore, the reproduction of owner means the reproduction of rights, but does not mean the reproduction of those useful properties of production factors for which the rights to use them are purchased. It should also be noted that, of course, nothing prevents the producer to buy the title of property too. But here he acts not as a producer and as an owner. This is just another feature that can be combined with the function of the producer.

This means that the reproduction of primary resources is reduced to consumption of consumer goods, i.e. of final products, needed for owners' life.[6] (See, Leiashvily, 1996, 2011, 2012). Of course this is the reproduction of

[6] "It is clear that in taking in food, for example, which is a form of consumption, the human being produces his own body. But this is also true of every kind of consumption which in one way

resources not in a physical, but in economic sense.[7] But, after all, economics is interested exactly in economic sense of economic processes. Also, production of final products is of interest for economics not as a physical or technological process, but as an economic process. Namely, it is interested in production process of final products *as commodities,* which belong to their owners, have social utility, are destined for sale, etc. But the producers and owners of final products as goods are entrepreneurs. Therefore, the reproduction of final product is unthinkable not only without consumption of primary resources, but without the reproduction of entrepreneurs' life too. Reproduction of their life is as much a necessary condition for economic reproduction of final products, as reproduction of life of production factors' owners is for economic reproduction of primary resources.

3. It follows that the sphere of consumption of final products is the sphere of reproduction of primary resources and the sphere of production of final products is the sphere of consumption of primary resources. Each of these sectors produces goods that are consumed by the opposite sector. A "resource" of one side is a "product" for the other side. Just because of this contradiction they become necessary for each other, becoming the necessary parts of wholeness. This wholeness, dissected inside into departments of economy, which in turn are composed of separate branches, just dictates the proportions of social production, consumption, distribution and exchange. This whole is a market economy "producing goods through the consumption of goods." And the relations between the production and consumption sectors, as the parts of a whole, take the form of market exchange.

As we see the "products" and "resources" are relative concepts. The economic goods simultaneously are products for their producers and resources for their consumers. Therefore, it is necessary to give a clear criterion for distinguishing these categories. For both production and consumption sectors "primary resource" is a good, which is consumed in given sector, but is produced - in another. The "final product," on the contrary, is produced in this sector and consumed in another. "Intermediate product (resource)" is produced and consumed in one and the same sector.[8] This also implies that primary income of one sector is the spending of opposite sector for the purchase of

---

or another produces human beings in some particular aspect. Consumptive production" (Marx, 1958, 716).

[7] Of course, in the physical sense, the amount of reproduced resources (services of production factors) depends on the amount of production factors, but not on the amount of products consumed by its owner.

[8] Below in the text to avoid confusion, commonly used "resources" and "products" are used called as resources and products for production sector.

goods produced in the first sector. Accordingly, for production sector the primary incomes are incomes from the sale of final products, but for consumption sector - incomes from the sale of services of production factors (i.e. salary, interest, rent and profit.).

4. Since production and consumption, essentially, are one and the same transformation process of some goods into other goods, then production and consumption economic sectors exhibit many similar features. So, to consumption sector, as to the sector of reproduction of primary resources, many of the concepts are applicable that are used in the analysis of production sector. In production sector firms transform primary resources into the final products. Respectively, they buy primary resources and sell final products. Analogous, but opposite role is carried out by households in consumption sector. They buy final products and sell primary resources and, consequently, in the economic sense, they transform final products into primary resources. As firms, producing the same product, form branches of economy, as well households, reproducing the same resources, represent the branches, providing production factors' services to producers. All actors (firms and households) and all branches of economy transform some goods into others, sell them to each other, receive incomes and make expenditures, they all need fixed and working capitals for normal functioning, etc.

5. The exchange ratios (prices) in the market are set so that only part of final product is exchanged for primary resources needed to produce that product. That is, the value of resources, spent in branches of production sector, is equal to the value of only one part of produced product. That part of produced product, which is exchanged for resources necessary for reproduction of whole product, is a *necessary product*. The value of the rest part of created product is *surplus product*, sales of which makes a profit and is the reward for entrepreneurial risk.[9] Similarly, only a part of primary resources is exchanged for final products required for reproduction of these resources (that is, to satisfy the owners' current living needs). This is the *necessary resource*. Accordingly, only one part of resources is necessary for payment of owners' current consumption. The rest part of resources is the *surplus* or *saved resource*, the sale of which generates owners' saving and which is the reward for his abstention and frugality. The more the owners' abstention is the more

[9] "... Sraffa's work ... provided a basis for a definitive demonstration that the theoretical analysis of wages, profits, and prices, within a surplus approach, was entirely independent of any 'labour theory of value' and, indeed, that any labour theory is necessarily a barrier to the development of a surplus-based theory" (Steadman, 1981, 12-13). "... a surplus approach to profits and prices has absolutely no need of any 'labour theory of value'" (Ibid,16).

resources are saved from their current consumption. That's why the total amount of reproduced resources depends only on the amount of production factors, which are in owners' possession, but not on the volume of their consumption.

Thus, during the reproduction process the necessary product and necessary resources are exchanged for each other. And as a result of their consumption some branches of economy reproduce surplus product, but other branches reproduce surplus (saved) resources. Thus, in each branch of economy the value of produced commodities is greater than the value of commodities consumed for their production. Within each branch surplus value is created (See: Leiashvily, 2012, 2011).

6. Surplus value is created both in the process of transformation of final products into the primary resources and in the transformation of primary products into the final products. In the first case it is done through abstinence, in the second - through entrepreneurship. Producer sells surplus products and makes profit and the owner sells the surplus (saved) resources and makes saving. Respectively, income and saving are the net income of economic subjects, the difference between incomes and expenditures which they received through entrepreneurship and abstinence. In its natural form the surplus product does not differ from the necessary product and it is sold in the market as well and at the same price as the necessary product is. If it had not been sold, it would not be a product at all, would not have value and would not bring a profit. Similarly, in its natural form surplus resource does not differ from a necessary resource. It is sold in the resource market as well and at the same price as a necessary resource is. Due to this saving are formed.

Moreover, since the primary resources exist only in the form of production factors' services, i.e. in the form of a process, which occurs over time (which is irreversible), the saving of these resources is possible only in the form of money obtained by selling them or is materialized form (work in process, finished products). In other words, saving of primary resources means abstaining not from their use at all, but from their use to meet current needs and, therefore, implies their use for investing them in one form or another.

7. Proportions, in which the product *prices* are divided into the costs and profit, correspond to the proportions, in which the *amount* of produced products is divided into necessary and surplus products. And the proportions, in which the resource *prices* are divided into consumption expenditure and saving, correspond to the proportions in which *amount* of reproduced

resources are divided into necessary and surplus resources.[10] Ultimately, it appears that consumers pay for the final product more than producers spend for its production and producers pay for the primary resource more than consumers (owners) spent for its reproduction. But where is the source of payment for surplus product and for surplus resource? Who is their buyer?

8. The sources of payment for surplus product, from which the entrepreneurs' profit derives, are the entrepreneurs profits themselves. Since entrepreneurs themselves are also the consumers, buying the final products from their incomes (just what their profits are). That is they buy a part of their products from each other as well as all other consumers buy products from them. And the sources of payment of surplus resource, from which the consumers' saving are formed, are their saving themselves. Saving are those free money resources, which through money market are transformed into credit resources for production investments. And this is the source of payment for surplus resource. That is, surplus resource is bought by entrepreneurs, but they buy them with borrowed monetary resources, which are formed from saving of the owners of these resources. Thus, the saving, transformed into credit resources for investment, additionally enter the resources market. And the profits of the whole class of entrepreneurs, consuming products, additionally enter the product market. In addition the government buys surplus products and surplus resources. That is, they are paid from the state budget and, consequently, from the taxes that are part of the same profits and saving.

2. Physical, Human, Public and Natural Capital

1. As we see, the necessary products and resources are directly involved in reproduction process of each other and their functions in this process are clear. But what is the function of surplus products and resources? To answer this question you first need to clarify some circumstances.

In the process of reproduction of final products, not only primary resources are consumed and in the process of reproduction of primary resources not only final products are consumed. The capital goods are also

[10] Since profit is generated from the value of surplus product, the surplus value is a part of the value added. Another part of value added is the value of necessary product, which corresponds to wages, interest and rent.

consumed.[11] The times, during which the various goods are consumed and reproduced, differ from each other. Depending on whether you need for consumption of goods more or less time than the conditional unit of time (usually a year), the goods are divided into *durable (capital) and nondurable goods*. This applies to all branches of economy either of production or consumption sector. Therefore, the goods of both production and consumption use are divided into durable and nondurable goods.[12]

Along with the increase or decrease of time unit, some of the durable goods become nondurables or vice versa. That is, the difference between them is conditional and depends on the length of the period considered as the time unit. Distinction criteria between them is only in the fact that during this period nondurable goods are consumed completely, but durable goods in the same period are consumed only partially (See: Walras, 2000, 151-152). The total consumption and wear of the durable goods takes place over a longer period, covering a lot of time periods. Naturally, if during the period under consideration the good is not consumed completely and does not disappear along with consumption, we can only talk about its *depreciation* and *services*.

2. Broadly speaking, capital is a good, use of which provides useful services, allows increase of production of goods, and generates incomes. Both for production of products and for reproduction of resources (in consumption sector), physical, human, natural and public capitals are required. All of them are able to provide appropriate services of both production and consumption use. However, the durables are worn out during their use. They have to be restored. Consequently, the consumption of capital should be distinguished from the consumption of its services. Capital services are consumed and disappear entirely in consumption process, while the capital wears out only gradually over a long period of time. However, while the capital exists and functions, it is able to deliver the services. Therefore, not the service of capital, but the capital itself needs physical reproduction. The capital services by

[11] Various kinds of capital are nothing else than the factors of production (See: Walras, 2000, 150-151). Instead of traditional and vague notions of "Capital", "Labor", "Land", in modern literature are increasingly used the concepts "physical, human and natural capital."

[12] Regarding services of capital (production factors in his terminology), Walras wrote: "They are of two kinds. There are such services that are absorbed as such during the private or social public consumption ... We call them consumable services. And there are those which are transformed by agriculture, industry, trade into the incomes or capitals, i.e., into the products: such are the land fertility, labor of worker, the use of machines, machine tools, and tool. We will call them productive service" (Walras, 2000, 151-152). Accordingly, capital goods themselves can be divided into capital goods for production purposes and for consumer purposes.

themselves do not need the reproduction;[13] they are reproduced together with the operation of capital. Reproduction of services is reduced only to ensure the normal operation of capital, which in turn needs certain costs. Another matter is a capital itself. For its restoration it is necessary to invest (as depreciation) the part of goods, produced by it, into its reproduction. It also follows that the costs for restoration of the capital should be distinguished from the costs for its operation.[14] These differences between the durable and nondurable goods determine a number of significant features of economic activity.

3. *Physical capital.* Since nondurable goods are consumed entirely within the year, then the reproduction of these goods also has to be performed annually. That is, they are reproduced in the same rhythm in which they are consumed. But since the physical capital is consumed during the year only partially, the reproduction and replacement of the old capital by the new one takes place only after full depreciation of the old capital. It should be noted that in *production sector*, for primary resources, entrepreneur pays only for capital services, but not for consumption of capital itself. But, as has already been noted, not only services are consumed in production process, but also the capital itself – in the form of depreciation. And entrepreneur has to compensate this depreciation to the owner at his own expense.[15] But it is not possible to determine exactly either what the share of current depreciation of capital is, or after how many years it will be depreciated completely. Therefore, no one compensates and cannot compensate to the owners of capital the current expenditures of capital (but not the services). It is possible to compensate only entire capital after its physical or moral depreciation. Replacing of depreciated capital by the new one is just the payment for the capital consumption. Therefore, consumption of capital in contrast to consumption of its services is not the current consumption, but the *consumption in debt.* And in parallel to this depreciation, entrepreneurs accumulate money for future replacement of physically or morally depreciated capital. These funds are invested in production of new physical capital. So it turns out that in conditions of equilibrium, consumption of physical capital in debt should be accompanied by parallel investment in its reproduction.

[13] Only the right of use of these services needs reproduction which, as noted, is reduced to reproduction of subjects of law (owners).

[14] For the functioning of physical and natural capital, expenditures of energy, lubricants, fertilizers, irrigation, etc. are required, and for the functioning of human capital, the consumption of final products, creation of conditions for labor, etc. are necessary.

[15] If the entrepreneur is the owner himself, he has to repay that depreciation to himself. Otherwise, his property will decrease.

In consumption sector, consumers, in addition to nondurables, also consume durables (apartment, car, household appliances). If consumers and owners of these goods are different subjects, consumers pay for the services of these goods in accordance with market price, which covers the cost of depreciation. In this case, the restoration of capital is performed by its owner. But if the good belongs to consumer, even though he does not pay for its services (pays to himself), parallel to consumption of this good he has to save and invest money for its replacement after its depreciation. But until the replacement of capital goods by the new one, he consumes it in debt to himself in the sense that if he does not cover the debt, then his property will decrease by the amount of the value of depreciated capital.

4. *The human capital.* For manufacturing of product not only physical, but also human capital is necessary. Human capital is the ability of man to intellectual and physical labor, the ability to perform different economic functions (entrepreneurship, ownership, investment, etc.).[16] Due to realization of these abilities a person creates economic values. In other words, human capital is the stock of knowledge, skills, experience, training, health, social relations, etc, by which he is able to perform certain economic functions. All this is not accumulated only during the investment process, but it also morally and materially wears. That is, usual conventional depreciation approach can be applied to the human capital. It is formed by investment in improving the level and quality of human life, including - education, training, health, in development of entrepreneurial, creative and communication skills as well as in science, culture and art, recreation, living conditions and other components of human capital (See: Shultz, 1971).

And all these features, knowledge and ability exist only in a living man, healthy, educated, working and living in a normal environment. This means that the existence and functioning of human capital implies current consumption of final products for the maintenance of normal living conditions. But during the operation this very capital also wears out. The knowledge and experience become obsolete over time, people get sick, temporarily or permanently lose work capacity, when reaching retirement age withdraws from the labor force, etc. And, finally, just die, for a man is mortal.

[16] Frugality, abstinence is a similar form of manifestation of human capital services as the entrepreneurship, physical and intellectual labor. Payment for labor is wage, for entrepreneurship - profit and for abstinence - saving. Human capital as well as physical capital is needed for the operation of both, sector of product reproduction and resource reproduction. Entrepreneurship creates a new value, and abstinence saves it. Only in this way the wealth accumulation and property increase is possible.

Accordingly, it is necessary to renew the knowledge and experience, to restore health, raise and educate the younger generation for the inflow of new workforce, raise the heirs of property, successors of business, etc. All this requires the economic costs and implies consumption of final products by above the necessary costs for current consumption of owners of human capital.[17] It is necessary to accumulate funds for education, sickness, to create the insurance and pension funds, etc. This means - to make saving from incomes and, therefore, to limit the current consumption. Some of these saving are used as a kind of "depreciation allowances" for recovery and some for the net investment in human capital.

5. *Public capital.* Operation of economic subjects is impossible without production and consumption of public goods, such as security, justice, rule of law, health, education, transport and communication facilities, power and water supply, radio and television broadcasting, street lighting, etc. All this is public capital and its services. Public capital is a set of state assets. Public goods are non-excludable and non-rivalrous. So they cannot be paid by private actors, they have no market price. Public capital services are free for society, because the public capital belongs to whole society; the government only manages it on behalf of society and in its interest. Accordingly, in their economic sense, taxes paid by economic subjects are not the prices or payment for public goods. Taxes are forcibly withdrawn part of incomes, needed for reproduction and functioning of public capital. In other words, taxes are forced saving, which serve for investment in public capital, as well as depreciation - for investment in physical capital. Taxes are paid by both producers and consumers, because they both use services of public capital. Thus, the public capital is the unity of those parts of physical and human capital, which are formed and operate due to forced saving and investment by all members of society and which is jointly and free of charge consumed by whole society. And taxes are forced saving that are invested in public capital.

6. *Natural capital.* Exceeding the permissible level of exploitation of nature has resulted in that the global economy consumes not only the services of natural capital, but also the natural capital itself. Destruction of nature has reached scales at which the nature cannot recover itself by natural processes and keep the ecological balance. But the costs for restoration of wear of natural capital are insufficient. The environmental crisis just is the intensified "wear" of natural capital. To put it in economic terms, depreciation allowances for investment in natural capital have lagged behind the rate of wear of

[17] I.e. excess of the cost for operation of human capital.

capital.[18] Like the restoration of physical, human and public capital, the natural capital also must be restored.[19] But no matter from where is funded this process (from the state budget or from international funds), in any case, the economic sense of this process also reduces to investment of some portion of the surplus product and resource in restoration of capital.

Rent, which entrepreneurs pay to the owners of natural capital, is the payment for services of this capital, but not the depreciation on its restoration. Restoration of natural capital is a problem that cannot be solved at the level of individual owner. It requires coordinated efforts at the state and international level. This means that the depreciation expense for restoration of natural capital is mainly made from government or international funds. This, in turn, means that eventually, these funds are generated from the same taxes as the public capital is. Therefore, further in the text, referring to public capital and taxes, we mean also natural capital and investment in its restoration.

3. PROFIT, SAVING, INVESTMENT AND CONSUMPTION IN DEBT

1. In reproduction of both products and resources, except of nondurable goods, the physical, human and public capital is consumed. But consumption of capital goods, as opposed to consumption of nondurables, is consumption in debt, in which capital wears. For restoration of worn and for net increase of capital, in parallel to consumption, it is necessary to set aside from incomes the means for investment in production of new capital. But to put off these means is possible only from that part of income, which is not consumed. Thus, the only source of investment in physical, human and public capital for producers is the gross profit, and for consumers - gross saving. But because they are formed from surplus product and surplus resource, in reality the surplus product and surplus resources are invested.

2. However, this investment is veiled. The surplus products and resources are bought and sold on the market along with all the other products. As a result

---

18 According to P. Hawken and others, the next industrial revolution "depends on the . . . investing in natural capital, or restoring and sustaining natural resources" (See: Hawken, 1999), http://en.wikipedia.org/wiki/Natural_capital#cite_ref-nat_1-0.

19 "Of greater concern for some countries is that standard depreciation measures have not taken into account the degradation in quality of the natural environment. There have been various attempts to widen the scope of depreciation to reflect environmental degradation (or improvements, if such is the case), but without much success" (Stiglitz, 2009, 24).

of their sales, profits and saving are generated. But profit and saving, as monetary resources, free from current expenditure, is the formation source for all monetary funds (private, municipal and state budgets, depreciation, insurance, pension funds, etc.). But, in the end, from these funds the surplus resources and products are again bought, just from which the physical, human and public capitals are produced.[20] Money itself cannot produce the capital goods. It requires products and resources. Investing just means that part of the products and resources is used not for production and consumption of nondurable goods, but for production and subsequent consumption of capital goods.

3. Just as production and consumption of nondurable goods is mediated by their exchange for money, also production and consumption of capital goods is mediated by the formation and use of funds. But if you ignore the “monetary veil,” there are invested namely surplus resources and products as goods free from current consumption. So, from reproduction viewpoint it turns out that some subjects sold surplus products and resources on the market (while creating money assets) and others buy them (spending money assets). That is, in the end, there is a usual exchange of goods in the market. Therefore, a simple reproduction implies equilibrium between production and consumption not just of necessary, but also of surplus products and resources.

As we see, investment of profits and saving in physical, human and public capital is only a monetary reflection of real investment of surplus resources and products. In this case, for an adequate understanding of reproduction process, it is crucial to realize the intrinsic relationships between gross profit and gross saving, as well as between gross investment and gross consumption in debt.

4. *Profit and saving.* The transformation of some products into another in a market economy takes place. In result of these transformations and further exchange of goods the profit remains in production sector, and the saving remains in consumption sector. But since the production and consumption sectors are interconnected through market exchange, then profit and saving are also internally interconnected. In fact, the alternation of incomes and expenditures takes place in both production and consumption spheres. Producers' incomes are consumers' expenditures and producers' expenditures are consumers' incomes. Accordingly, the difference between incomes and expenditures takes for them the mirror opposite forms of profit and saving.

---

[20] Or directly capital goods are bought. But before we buy them, someone has to produce them. They may be produced only from surplus products and saved resources.

That is why the gross profit and saving are internally interconnected. As soon as incomes of some are expenditures of others and vice versa, the profit and saving cannot be independent variables. Changing of exchange proportions between the final products and primary resources (i.e. their relative prices) has effect on the profits and saving in opposite way. Naturally, in conditions of equilibrium prices the gross profit and gross saving should match (See: Leiashvily, 2011, 2012).

5. It should be emphasized that the depreciation is a *part of profit*, but not a part of cost of product, which is slowly included into finished products. Depreciation allowance is a purely financial procedure that has very little relevance to real loss of value by fixed capital. The choice of norms and methods of depreciation depends on the economic policy of government, and not on the actual depreciation of capital. Disputes always arise in regard to the understanding of depreciation. There are two substantial descriptions of depreciation - (1) wearing of property and (2) building of the fund of its renovation. Uniform distribution of amortization during the different periods does not correspond to the actual processes of wear, because the older the object is, the faster it wears out. But it is impossible to determine the adequacy of real wear to depreciation rates. In addition, any depreciation rate implies the possibility of exploitation of object after its complete normative wear. Setting the depreciation rate, useful life or procedure for calculating depreciation, government regulates the pace and nature of reproduction in the industry. Thus, the depreciation is a part of profit, which is not subject to tax and from which no dividends are paid, but it is not the extended writing-off of previously incurred expenditures.

6. To be able to carry on business, entrepreneurs should not only buy the primary resources, but also invest in their personal consumption. These investments are investments in their own human capital. These are entrepreneurial skills, realization of which is just a service of this capital. Society pays him for entrepreneurial services. Profit is this payment and at the same time, confirmation of social utility of this services. From an entrepreneur's viewpoint his activity is for him a use of human capital belonging to him, which brings him an income in the form of profit. But the human capital exists only in a living person, living and acting in normal conditions. Therefore, the current consumption of final products for supporting conditions of living and activity is a necessary condition for the existence and functioning of this capital. Unlike consumption of owners, entrepreneurs' consumption is consumption in debt. For in contrast to owners, who pay for their current consumption out of the previously obtained incomes,

entrepreneurs only invest funds from their monetary assets without knowing in advance whether its consumption expenditure will be compensated by the results of his activity.[21] That is, he consumes in debt from future income. In this regard the thought of Smith is interesting:

> "His profit, besides, is his revenue, the proper fund of his subsistence. As, while he is preparing and bringing the goods to market, he advances to his workmen their wages, or their subsistence; so he advances to himself, in the same manner, his own subsistence, which is generally suitable to the profit which he may reasonably expect from the sale of his goods. Unless they yield him this profit, therefore, they do not repay him what they may very properly be said to have really cost him" (Smith, 1977, p. 56).

An advance, Smith writes about, is rather investment in human capital of entrepreneur.

7. Producer, thanks to expenditures, receives incomes and the consumer - thanks to incomes carries expenditures. Producers first carry expenditures, then receive incomes. Consumers – vice versa. Accordingly, the subject as a producer makes economic decisions regarding expenditures, depending on the incomes expected in future, but as a consumer - depending on the previously received incomes. Therefore, the profit making is associated with entrepreneurial risk and the making of saving - with thriftiness.

Society as a whole, as well as each economic subject, individually and simultaneously is producer and consumer. Therefore, in both capacities it simultaneously is both entrepreneur, and saver. Producer is not only an entrepreneur, but also a "saver," because he does not spend received income entirely for the continuation of production but saves a part of income. Just this «saving» is withdrawn profit. And making decision about spending, producer calculates not only profit expected from future incomes, but also - what "saving" will remain from previous incomes, i.e., also takes into account the amount of profit remaining for withdrawal. Also, consumers are not only saver, but also "entrepreneur." For taking decision regarding the current expenditures he takes into account not only which saving will remain from the past income at the end of the current period, but also whether there will be

[21] In its economic sense, consumption of final products, necessary both for operation and for reproduction of entrepreneurs' human capital, is consumption in debt. Whereas consumption in debt for owners implies only the reproduction of human capital, but its operation (through which the primary resources are reproduced) implies a current consumption.

excess of future income above the current expenditure, i.e. whether will be "profit."

Therefore, all economic actors make each decision regarding expenditures taking into account both received and expected income. Consequently, the decision is taken from the position of both savers and entrepreneurs. Since in general case the excess of expected income above current expenditure is his profit, then excess of already received income above the current expenditures is saving. And in the alternation of incomes and expenditures from subject's position depends whether the difference between incomes and expenditures will be considered as profit, or - as saving. That is "entrepreneur" and "saver," "profit" and "saving" are the same reflective concepts as the concept of "producer" and "consumer" (See: Leiashvily, 2012, 98-99).

8. *Investment and consumption in debt.* Investment is the transformation of income into capital.[22] But naturally, only that part of income can be transformed in capital, which is not consumed, i.e. saving or profit. Marx believed that investments are made only out of profits, and Keynes - only from saving. But actually investments are made from both, that is, from net income of economic agents. However, profits and saving are money. But money cannot produce real capital goods (whether physical, human or public capital). Money can create only money capital. Production of real capital goods requires real goods (products and resources). But in relation to real goods the same logic remains valid. As it has already been mentioned, it is possible to transform into capital goods (use to produce the capital goods) only those products and resources, which are not used in current consumption. Such are only surplus products and resources. Thus, investment is an investment of surplus products and resources into production of capital goods. Accordingly, the investor is one, who invests products and resources free from current consumption into production of capital goods. But one, who produces capital goods, consumes these products and resources in debt. Producer of capital goods and investor may be different subjects or the same subject, but in any case production of capital goods and investments - are different, but closely interrelated economic functions. One thing is clear that the reverse side of investment is consumption in debt.[23]

---

[22] ". . . broadly speaking, new investment . . . ., means the purchase of a capital asset of any kind out of income" (Keynes, 1977) (http://www.marxists.org/reference/subject/ economics /keynes/general-theory/ch07.htm).

[23] The economic sense of this process is that the investor provides his resources in credit to producer of capital, but the producer consumes these resources in debt. As debt is the reverse side of credit, consumption in debt is the reverse side of investment as well.

9. In a barter. economy investment and consumption in debt are linked with each other as inextricably as selling and buying. In a barter exchange, buying and selling of goods are fused into a single process. When money appears as a mediator, buying and selling are disconnected in time and space as two separate acts. However, since the sale is made possible without buying and buying without selling, the delay or acceleration in trade is connected with removal or involvement of money in circulation. Accordingly, the monetary assets increase or decrease. Similar changes occur in the process of investment and consumption in debt of surplus product and surplus resources. With appearing of money the process of investment and consumption in debt also separate from each other. Additional processes of investment and consumption in debt of money capital arise between them. The surplus products and surplus resources first should be sold in the market and get money form of profit and saving. Money capital is formed from profits and saving. That is, part of money income is invested in a money capital, which will then be invested in production of real capital, i.e., surplus product and surplus resources will again be purchased for production of capital. Thus, investment in real capital is related to the divestment of money capital.

But the gap in time is between formation of money capital and its transformation into a real capital, during which the money capital can provide a variety of financial services and earn interest. Money capital earns money income and begins an independent life. Moreover, with the development of market economy these processes grow in a complicated world of finance, which functions according to its own laws (See: Toporowski 2002, Hudson 2010). Various intermediary financial institutions (banks, credit unions, insurance companies, pension funds, stock exchanges, etc.) appear with their financial instruments (currency, securities, bonds, futures, options, etc.). And though this world of finance acquires enormous power over the economic life of society, it is based on the processes of real economy. The real and money sectors of economy are a single system. Therefore, if equilibrium is disturbed in one sector between investment and consumption in debt, the equilibrium will be disturbed in another sector too.

10. Just as the reverse side of current production is current consumption, the reverse side of investment is consumption in debt (See: Leiashvily, 2011, 2012). They are inextricably linked to each other. If what is invested is not consumed in debt (and therefore capital is not produced), then such investment is not investment. If consumption in debt serves only to increasing of current consumption without creation of capital, it means that in future there will be divestment. For after the expiration, the debt should be returned with interest.

This means that in the future agent will have to withdraw funds from the existing capital. So, investment and consumption in debt are two aspects of one and the same process of reallocation of production and consumption possibilities among economic actors. This redistribution of opportunities *between the subjects* for the subjects themselves is a means of *redistribution in time* of production and consumption possibilities in order to optimize their activity. But in a market economy, each subject produces commodities for others and he consumes commodities produced by others. In conditions when ones produce commodities and others consume them, misbalance is possible between production and consumption. The same can be said about investment and consumption in debt. In a market economy, some invest commodities (surplus product and resources) and others - consume them in debt. So, misbalance between them is possible, which leads to the disorder of economy.

11. The whole sense of investment is that investment of part of the income in capital allows increasing the capital. But the greater the capital is, the greater income it generates, which, in turn, allows more to save and invest and even more to increase capital, etc. That is capital is a self-expanding value (Marx). But if this process is not regulated and occurs spontaneously, then on the macro level disparities are inevitable between economic flows, such as profit, saving, investment and consumption in debt. This causes a disturbance of macroeconomic equilibrium and generates business cycles.

12. But the colorful variety of manifestation of turbulent financial life should not be misleading and hinder the identification of intrinsic relationship between the real processes of economic reproduction - production and consumption, distribution and exchange, investment and consumption in debt. It is clear that investment and consumption in debt involves withdrawal of excess economic goods (opportunities) from one time interval and from one subject and brings them to another time interval and another subject. But society's capacity is limited by available resources and technologies. Therefore, to maintain equilibrium in economy, if one consumes more, then someone else should consume less; if someone consumes in debt, someone else should invest in order to compensate it. If a private subject or a society today invests more than it consumes in debt, then tomorrow it will be able to increase consumption. Conversely, if it consumes more in debt than invests (eats through capital), tomorrow it will have to reduce consumption. That is, the waves of economic activity are generated.

If we collect all of the above arguments and reflect on the dialectic relationships of all economic processes in the focus of a single system of market economy, we inevitably come to the understanding that the economy is a operationally closed self-organized system of recursive processes. Due to the circular organization of economic processes the economic system has several unique properties that have been well studied in synergetic, constructivism, second-order cybernetics, and in the theory of recursive operations. Therefore, interdisciplinary analysis of these processes allows answering the many unresolved questions of economic theory.

Operational closeness of market economy becomes particularly evident in the formalization of these processes by means of mathematical modeling. The following is a "symmetric model" of general economic equilibrium, analysis of which will greatly facilitate the identification of hidden regularities of functioning of closed decentralized economic system.

Chapter 3

"SYMMETRIC MODEL" OF ECONOMIC EQUILIBRIUM

1. MODEL OF GENERAL EQUILIBRIUM

1. This model reflects a system of interrelations not between economic agents, but between those economic flows, processes, functions that ensure the integrity of the economic system. Here is considered a decentralized closed economic system in which final products (m) are produced through consumption of primary resources (n) and primary resources (n) are reproduced through consumption of final products (m). In order to simplify the model, the intermediate products aren't considered.[24] Since both products and resources are the goods, the market economy is represented as a system in which "production of commodities by means [of consumption] of commodities" takes place (P. Sraffa). Division of goods into products and resources is conditional. Therefore, all goods are the products for their producers and resources - for their consumers. The sector 1 produces products that are resources for the sector 4. In result of consumption of these resources, the sector 4 produces products that are resources for the sector 1. Exchange of goods happens in the markets (sectors 2 and 3). All goods are produced by ones and consumed by others, some sell and others buy. Therefore, all agents are both – producers and consumers, sellers and buyers. Each of them receives

[24] When taking into account that the intermediate production model will take a more complicated form, although functionally closeness of system and the very essence of the processes do not change (See, Appendix 2).

incomes and bears expenditures, and the difference between revenues and expenditures is used for investment in physical and human capital.

Generation of incomes and expenditures is based on the price. As the expenditures of buyers are incomes for sellers, we have the following. On the one hand, prices reflect production costs and therefore are formed on the basis of the prices of goods consumed in production processes, on the other, the prices reflect the utility of goods. Since the utility is the ability to satisfy the solvent needs, the prices stipulate the amount of those expenditures that consumers sacrifice from their incomes for the purchase of this utility. That is, the price of the purchased goods for consumers is monetary expenditures caused by the purchase of one good. Therefore, in this model, the incomes and prices paid from these incomes have opposite signs. This reflects the fact that in result of buying, the prices of goods "neutralize" incomes, at the same time the utility "neutralizes" (satisfies) the need as a result of its consumption. The elements of diagonal of matrix simultaneously show production value of goods as well as their consumption value. Since the elements of diagonal of matrix simultaneously are the elements of both rows and columns, they simultaneously reflect both costs and utility. Lines show the elements of the cost of production of goods, and the columns - the distribution and consumption of the same goods in the production processes of other goods.

In the matrix the resources clockwise are transformed into products, which in turn are consumed as resources for the production of other products, etc. The money incomes are transformed counterclockwise into money expenditures, which in turn are themselves the incomes and then again are transformed into expenditures, etc. Each element of the diagonal aligns the rows and columns of the matrix. Sum of elements in each row of the sector 1 is equal to the sum of elements of corresponding columns of sector 4, and the sum of elements in each row of the sector 4 is equal to the sum of elements of corresponding columns of sector 1. That is, in a closed economic system under equilibrium conditions, is produced only what is consumed and is consumed only what is produced. This correspondence between production and consumption means that for each commodity (products and resources), demand and supply, selling and buying fully correspond to each other.

Table 1. Matrix of closed economic system

Sector 1 **Sector 2**

$-a_{11}x_1v_1$	$-a_{12}x_1v_2$	...	$-a_{1(n-1)}x_1v_{(n-1)}$	$-\alpha_1 A_1$					x_1p_1
$-a_{21}x_2v_1$	$-a_{22}x_2v_2$	...	$-a_{2(n-1)}x_2v_{(n-1)}$	$-\alpha_2 A_2$				x_2p_2	
...	...	...	...	...			...		
$-a_{(m-1)1}x_{(m-1)}v_1$	$-a_{(m-1)2}x_{(m-1)}v_2$	...	$-a_{(m-1)(n-1)}x_{(m-1)}v_{(n-1)}$	$-\alpha_{(m-1)} A_{(m-1)}$		$x_{(m-1)}p_{(m-1)}$			
$-a_{m1}x_mv_1$	$-a_{m2}x_mv_2$	...	$-a_{m(n-1)}x_mv_{(n-1)}$	$-\alpha_m A_m$ $-P'$	x_mp_m $I = S$				
				$P = Q$ y_nv_n	$-S'$ $-\beta_n B_n$	$-b_{n(m-1)}p_{(m-1)}y_n$	...	$-b_{n2}p_2y_n$	$-b_{n1}p_1y_n$
			$y_{(n-1)}v_{(n-1)}$		$-\beta_{(n-1)}B_{(n-1)}$	$-b_{(n-1)(m-1)}y_{(n-1)}p_{(m-1)}$	...	$-b_{(n-1)2}y_{(n-1)}p_2$	$-b_{(n-1)1}y_{(n-1)}p_1$
		...			...	...	...	...	...
	y_2v_2				$-\beta_2 B_2$	$-b_{2(m-1)}y_2p_{(m-1)}$	...	$-b_{22}y_2p_2$	$-b_{21}y_2p_1$
y_1v_1					$-\beta_1 B_1$	$-b_{1(m-1)}y_1p_{(m-1)}$	...	$-b_{12}y_1p_2$	$-b_{11}y_1p_1$

Sector 3 **Sector 4**

$\mathbf{x_i}$ - goods produced in sector 1 (consumed in sector 4), $i = 1,2, \ldots, m$;

$\mathbf{p_i}$ - value of goods x_i (equilibrium price), $i = 1,2, \ldots, m$;

$\mathbf{y_j}$ - goods produced in sector 4 (consumed in the sector 1), $j = 1,2, \ldots, n$;

$\mathbf{v_j}$ - value of the goods y_j (equilibrium price), $j = 1,2, \ldots, n$;

$\mathbf{a_{ij}}$ - consumption of recourse j for production of unit of product i (technological coefficients);

$\mathbf{b_{ji}}$ - consumption of product i for reproduction of unit of recourse j;

$\boldsymbol{\alpha}_i$ - the rate of surplus product (save resources) in the production of good i;

$\boldsymbol{\beta}_i$ - the rate of surplus product (save resources) in the production of good j;

P - gross surplus product (save resources) in the sector 1;

S - gross surplus product (save resources) in the sector 4;

Q - gross consumption in debt;
I - gross investment;
S’ - saving from consumption in debt;
P’ - surplus product (save resources) in the production of investment goods.

In the sector 1 as well as in the sector 4, the value of produced goods is greater than the sum of the values of goods consumed in the process of their production. As it has already been noted, all agents are both producers and consumers. If all economic agents are presented as producers of goods, the difference between the value of goods produced and consumed will take the form of surplus value. But if all agents are presented as consumers of goods, this difference will take the form of saved value. Accordingly, in the first case the surplus value is materialized into the surplus product and in the second case, the saved value is materialized into saved resources.[25] Agents are interested in increasing the surplus product and saved resource. Production of surplus product requires entrepreneurial risk, but for saving of resources abstinence is necessary.

Since each agent simultaneously is a producer, which produces the surplus product and the consumer, which saves resources, they simultaneously perform a function of entrepreneur as well as the function of saver.[26] Thus, in order to receive excess of value during the process of production and consumption of goods by the economic agents both risk and abstinence are needed. Reward for risk and abstinence is just the profits and saving.

2. Description of the model: Constants:

a_{ij}, b_{ji}. Variables: x_i , y_j , p_i , v_j , α_i , β_j..

1) If all the agents are presented as producers, then:

$$A_i = \sum a_{ij} x_i v_j ; \quad i = 1,2 ....m; \quad j = 1,2....(n - 1); \qquad (1)$$

$$B_j = \sum b_{ji} y_j p_i; \quad i = 1,2 ....(m - 1); \; j = 1,2....n; \qquad (2)$$

$$(1+ \alpha_i) \sum a_{ij} v_j = p_i; \quad i = 1,2 ....m; \quad j = 1,2....(n - 1); \qquad (3)$$

$$(1+ \beta_j)\sum b_{ji} p_i = v_j ; \quad i = 1,2 .. ..(m - 1); \; j = 1,2....n; \qquad (4)$$

---

[25] It should be added that the primary resources saved in sector 4 are saved from their use for current consumption and not from the consumption in general. They are used for investment and, therefore, are consumed in the production of capital goods (depreciation and net increase of capital) and inventory. For primary resources are services of production factors. But the services cannot be saved in another way than in the form of goods produced by them (i.e. in materialized form) or in the form of money from selling of these goods.

[26] Since saving of primary resources is possible only in the form of investments, so the saving is associated with investment risk.

$$\sum a_{ij}\, x_i = y_j\,; \qquad j = 1,2\ ....(n - 1); \quad i = 1,2\ ....m; \tag{5}$$

$$\sum b_{ji}\, y_j = x_i\,; \qquad i = 1,2\ ....(m - 1); \quad i = 1,2\ ....m; \tag{6}$$

$$\alpha_0 = \frac{\sum_i \alpha_i A_i}{\sum_i A_i} \qquad i = 1,2\ ....m; \tag{7}$$

$$\beta_0 = \frac{\sum_j \beta_j B_j}{\sum_j B_j} \qquad j = 1,2....n; \tag{8}$$

$$x_i \geq x_{min}; \quad i = 1,2\ ....m; \quad y_j \leq y_{max}; \; j = 1,2....n. \tag{9}$$

2) If all the agents are presented as consumers, then:

$$A_i = x_i\, p_i\,; \qquad i = 1,2\ ....m; \tag{10}$$

$$B_j = y_j\, v_j\,; \qquad j = 1,2....n; \tag{11}$$

$$\sum a_{ij}\, v_j\, /(1-\alpha_i) = p_i; \quad i = 1,2\ ....m; \quad j = 1,2....(n - 1); \tag{12}$$

$$\sum b_{ji}\, p_i\, /(1-\beta_j) = v_j\,; \quad i = 1,2\ ....(m - 1); \; j = 1,2....n; \tag{13}$$

$$\sum a_{ij}\, x_i = y_j\,; \qquad j = 1,2\ ....(n - 1); \quad i = 1,2\ ....m; \tag{14}$$

$$\sum b_{ji}\, y_j = x_i\,; \qquad i = 1,2\ ....(m - 1); \quad i = 1,2\ ....m; \tag{15}$$

$$\alpha_0 = \frac{\sum_i \alpha_i x_i p_i}{\sum_i x_i p_i}\,; \qquad i = 1,2\ ....\ m; \tag{16}$$

$$\beta_0 = \frac{\sum_j \beta_j y_j v_j}{\sum_j y_j v_j}\,; \qquad j = 1,2\ ....\ n; \tag{17}$$

$$x_i \geq x_{min}; \quad 1,2\ ....m; \quad y_j \leq y_{max}\,; \; j = 1,2....n; \tag{18}$$

As we see, according to these formulas in both cases, the equilibrium price and the equilibrium quantity of goods are formed on the basis of recursive processes, and the equilibrium condition is equality: $P = Q = I = S$, and hence equality of average rate of profit α_0 and the average rate of saving β_0. Under competitive conditions α_0 and β_0 strive for equality and thereby cause a tendency toward equality $P = Q = I = S$ and thus to equilibrium of entire system.

Technological coefficients are the coefficients of transformation of primary resources into final products, and consumer coefficients – of final products into the primary resources. Prices are coefficients of exchange of money for goods and, accordingly, transformation coefficients of income into expenditures and expenditures - into incomes.

3. Under the conditions of equilibrium the gross profit is equal to gross consumption in debt (P = Q), and gross savings - to gross investment (S = I). Under equilibrium conditions, the leakage from producers' incomes in the form of withdrawn profits P, must be compensated by the inflow of funds in the form of loans for productive investments I. But leakage of funds from consumers' incomes in the form of savings S must be offset by inflows of funds for the financing of consumption in debt Q. That is, in the market of resources the condition of maintenance of demand at the appropriate level is the equality P = I, but on the market of products such condition is the equality S = Q. Otherwise, the balance between supply and demand (at current prices) is violated in the resource market as well as on the product market. But what is leaked from the sector 4 in the form of savings S under equilibrium conditions must be equal to that, which through the money market inflows into the sector 1 in the form of productive investments I. And what is in the form of withdrawn profits P outflows from the sector 1, should be equal to that which in the form of consumption in debt (consumer investment) Q inflows into the sector 4. This is reflected in the model, according to which production investments (investments in physical capital) I and gross savings S correspond to the same element of diagonal of the sector 2. Therefore, under equilibrium conditions I = S. Similarly, the consumer investment (investment in human capital, or consumption in debt) Q and gross profit P correspond to the same element of diagonal of the sector 3. Therefore, P = Q.

The equilibrium condition is the equality P = S = I = Q. So it must have equality $\alpha_0 = \beta_0 = r_0$, where α_0, β_0 and r_0, respectively, represent the average rate of profit, saving and interest. However, it should be noted that in contrast to all other commodity and money flows, transforming of P into Q, and transforming of S into I occurs not on the basis of equivalent exchange of goods, but on the basis of credit relations, in which the interest rate r_0 performs the balancing function.

Violation of equilibrium conditions in a system violates the equality between the sum of the elements of rows and corresponding columns. This leads to a bifurcation of the elements of diagonal. Discrepancies appear between production and consumption, supply and demand, cost and utility, production and consumption values. Deficient and surplus goods appear. In the markets of various goods will appear the unsold goods or idle money. Some get additional profit at the expense of losses of others or lost profits. This creates incentives to restore equilibrium in the markets. At the same time, the imbalance between any one pair of row and column, inevitably gives rise to an imbalance between other pairs of rows and columns. General economic equilibrium will not be achieved until reaching equality P = S = I = Q, which means that $\alpha_0 = \beta_0 = r_0$. The equilibrium states can be in infinite number in the conditions of different rates of interest and corresponding to them different values of gross profit, saving, investment and consumption in debt.

3. *Business cycles.* On the basis of "symmetric model" business cycle fluctuations can be interpreted as follows (See Figure 1). Under equilibrium conditions, the money flows flowing through tanks (resource market and product market) and the pressures in them are equal, since the leakage of money S and P balance each other as well as the flow of money I and D. Under such conditions, resources and products have the optimal prices. At these prices entrepreneurs receive a normal profit, which they consider as appropriate reward for the burden of entrepreneurial risk. The owners are doing normal savings satisfying them as payment for abstinence.

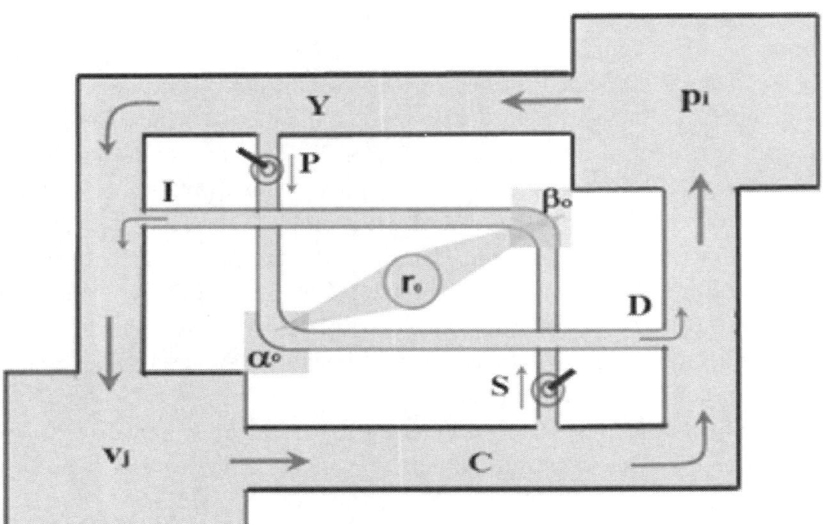

Figure 1. The scheme of circulation of financial flows.

In the phase of economic expansion in the economy the flows of incomes and expenditures increase. In result of Keynes psychological law the consumers' marginal propensity to save increases and the marginal propensity to consume decreases. As a consequence, in the general background of increasing of all money (and commodity) flows, in consumption sector the share of S increases, and the share of C decreases. On the other hand, as a result of formation of optimistic moods, the marginal propensity of producers to take risks increases. As a consequence of this opposite processes take place in production sector. The marginal propensity to expansion of production (to production consumption) increases and the marginal propensity to withdrawal of profits (to production saving) decreases. Accordingly, in general money flow the share of P decreases, while the share of Y increases.

The result of such redistribution of flows the "monetary pressure" in the upper tank (market products) decreases and in the lower tank (market resources) – increases. Accordingly, the relative prices of the products begin to decline and the relative prices of resources - to increase. But such changes in the system of prices provoke the phase change of economic cycle. A recession begins. The rate of profits is reduced, which leads to a decrease in propensity to take risk. As a result the production is reduced and the consumers' incomes and their propensity to save are reduced, etc. That is, arise opposite trends arise - the shares of S and Y are reduced, and the shares of P and C are growing. This leads to a redistribution of flow; the ratio of "money-pressures" in the markets of products and resources is reversed. The relative prices of products again begin to rise, and of resources - to decline. Recovery begins.

As a result of these fluctuations of economic activity the money supply required for service of transactions also fluctuates. In the phase of expansion the monetary resources are introduced in the circuit, and in the phase of recession – they are withdrawn. One should keep in mind that although the rate of profit received and withdrawn by producers are different, as well as the rates of saving received and withdrawn by consumers, but changing of the ratios of these norms in the process of expansion and recession causes only a redistribution of economic flows, but not the changes in the total money supply in the circuit. Input and output of financial resources occurs at the expense of monetary assets of economic subjects. And all these processes of input and output of money in circulation, or redistribution of cash flow depend directly on the level of interest rates. Level of r_0 effects the economic decisions and thus it effects P, S, I, D, α_0 and β_0. But P and S are the temporarily available money resources, which form the supply in the money market, and I and D form the demand for money. A supply and demand in the money market form the interest rate through which the economy seeks to restore the "golden ratio" $\alpha_0 = \beta_0 = r_0$ and, accordingly, restore the balance and the optimal ratios between the prices of resources and products.

In conditions of monetary economy the fluctuations of business cycle are the only mechanism that leads into conformity P, S, I and D (respectively, α_0, β_0 and r_0). But it does not provide equality, which is necessary for general equilibrium. It only keeps their divergences within certain limits. Decentralized economy is a system with "feedback," i.e. cause-and-effect relationships are closed in a circle and transformed into a functional relationship by which any deviation excites the forces for its self-elimination, which are proportional to the magnitude of this deviation. Natural laws of the market are "blindly" operating laws. The "blindness" is manifested in the fact that the uncontrolled self-stimulation and self-retardation of economy continues until they reach a critical turning points - a maximum production capacity and minimum consumption possibilities. Therefore, without government regulation of economy it is impossible in principle to eliminate cyclical fluctuations.

2. Information to Think

1. The "Symmetric model" is based on a dialectical analysis of the fundamental economic categories. This analysis has revealed such hidden relationships between economic phenomena and processes that are not visible at the empirical level. From the "symmetric model" reflecting these relationships, it is clear that economic processes form a closed system, and the functions performed by these processes are interdependent and have a circular organization. From a purely scientific point of view it is essential that the model of an economic system, built on the basis of half-forgotten and completely ignored by economists dialectical analysis and conclusions, drawn from the analysis of this model, correspond to the provisions and principles of constructivism and second-order cybernetics. That is, scientific conclusions and provisions, obtained by various methods and independently from each other, have turned out to be completely compatible. Below are a few quotes regarding the circular processes from the book «Understanding understanding» of the founder of second-order cybernetics H. von Foerster:

> "It seems that cybernetics is many different things to many different people. But this is because of the richness of its conceptual base; and I

believe that this is very good, otherwise cybernetics would become a somewhat boring exercise. However, all of those perspectives arise from one central theme; that of circularity. When, perhaps a half century ago, the fecundity of this concept was seen, it was sheer euphoria to philosophize, epistemologize, and theorize about its unifying power and its consequences and ramification on various fields" (Foerster, 2003, 288).

H. von Foerster leads to formulas x' = D (x, u), and u' = S (u, x) in which the variables x, y are represented as a function of themselves. It's also possible to take into account a period of time, if we introduce the parameter "time" in the form of an increasing sequence of time units: t now, t + 1, the following units of time: $x_t + 1 = D(x_t, u)$, and $u_t + 1 = S(u_t, x)$. He writes further:

"Those of you who are occupied with chaos theory and with recursive functions will recognize at once that these are the fundamental equations of recursive function theory. Those are the conceptual mechanisms with which chaos research is conducted; it is always the same equations over and over again. And they give rise to completely astonishing, unforeseen operational properties. Viewed historically, even early on one noticed a convergence to some stable values. An example: if you recursively take the square root of any random initial value (most calculators have a square root button), then you will very soon arrive at the stable value 1.0000. . . . No wonder, for the root of 1 is 1. The mathematicians at the turn of the century called these values the "Eigen values" of the corresponding functions (Ibid, 315).

It is easy to see that equations of "Symmetric model" reflect precisely that recursive function about which H. von Foerster writes and in which it is easy to "recognize at once that these are the fundamental equations of recursive function theory." Accordingly, the "Eigen values" in this model are the equilibrium prices and equilibrium quantity of goods in respect of which the actual prices and quantities fluctuate.

About 20 years ago there was an explosion of renewed interest in these recursive operations, as one discovered that many functions develop not only stable values but also a stable dynamic. One called these stabilities "attractors," apparently a leftover from a teleological way of thinking. Since one can let some systems march through the most diverse Eigen behaviors by making simple changes in the parameters, one soon stumbled onto a most interesting behavior that is launched by certain parametric values: the system rolls through a sequence of values without ever repeating one, and even if one believes one has taken one of these

> values as the initial value, the sequence of values cannot be reproduced: the system is chaotic (Ibid, 316).

To the 'Eigen behavior," about which von Foerster writes, within the economic system corresponds the algorithm of cyclical fluctuations of system relative to the equilibrium state, because these fluctuations are caused by the system itself, by intersystem endogenous factors. The environment makes only adjustments to the dynamics of these fluctuations, to the length of their phase, and to the amplitude of the waves, etc. But the impulses of environment are not the direct cause of these fluctuations.

> Through this recursive closure and only through this recursive closure do stabilities arise that could never be discovered through input/output analysis. What is fascinating is that while one can observe these stabilities it is in principle impossible to find out what generates these stabilities. One cannot analytically determine how this system operates, although we see that it does operate in a way that permits us to make predictions (Ibid, 316-317).

From the analysis of "Symmetric model" it may be concluded that the system tends to equilibrium in accordance with its internal nature. However, it is impossible to know exactly in which way this equilibrium has been achieved, which specific processes lead to it in a particular case, since one and the same state of equilibrium can be achieved by an infinite number of ways. That is, we know attractor, the state toward which the system tends, but it is impossible in principle to determine how it will be achieved.

As we can see, the mechanism of self-regulation of market economy is quite simple. This is a recursive process in a operationally closed system. To find out this has become possible only after the market economy has been presented as a operationally closed system of economic processes. But to present it in this form has become possible only in result of dialectical analysis of economic phenomena. This fact once again confirms the necessity of dialectical method for economic theory.

2. When in the early '50s K. Arrow, J. Debreu and independently of them L. Mackenzie have published their general equilibrium models, the mathematical direction of economic theory has received the new impetus to development. By intellectual efforts of these authors the foundation of modern mathematical models of decentralized economic system has been laid. For several decades a steady stream of works on the theory of general equilibrium has appeared. Some scientists have even considered the results obtained in this

field of science as one of the most significant achievements of mathematical branch of economic theory in the second half of the 20th century. This model has become an integral part of modern neoclassical paradigm. However, critics of this model rightly point out that, although, from a purely mathematical point of view, the existence of general equilibrium is really "gracefully" proved in it, but it is so abstract that is hardly seen through allusions to the economic reality.[27] Indeed, assumption on which the model is built, conditions for the existence of general equilibrium and the conclusions drawn from the model are completely unacceptable for an impartial scientific analysis. In an attempt to create an adequate model of general equilibrium, mathematical economists are so carried away with the purely mathematical side of the problem that involuntarily embark on the path "leading nowhere." For example, Mark Blaug writes:

> "The Arrow-Debreu paper provided a rigorous proof of the existence of multimarket equilibrium in a decentralized economy, ... This proof was rigorous by mathematical standards but it required some assumptions that clearly violated economic reality; for example, that there are forward markets for every commodity in all future periods and for all conceivable contingencies .... In short, the Arrow-Debreu proof had more to do with mathematical logic than with economics.... it has become a perfect example of what Ronald Coase has called "blackboard economics," a model that can be written down on blackboards using economic terms like "prices," "quantities," "factors of production," etc. but which nevertheless is palpably unrepresentative of any recognizable economic system" (Blaug, 1997, p.3).

The position of Steve Keen is similar to it:

> "It is almost superfluous to describe the core assumptions of Debreu's model as unrealistic: a single point in time at which all production and exchange for all time is determined; a set of commodities – including those which will be invented and produced in the distant future – which is known to all consumers; producers who know all the inputs that will ever be needed to produce their commodities ... " (Keen, 2011, p. 201).

[27] In this respect, the wording of official rationale of Nobel Prize awarded to Debreu in 1983 is interesting- "For his contributions to our understanding of the theory of general equilibrium and the conditions under which the general equilibrium exists in some abstract economy."

Arrow and Debreu have proved the theorem of existence of a general economic equilibrium by using the Kakutani theorem about fixed point. These fixed points, or otherwise "eigenvalues," exactly are the equilibrium prices that ensure the equilibrium of system. However, this method of proving the "existence theorem" became possible only under the absurd assumptions (only some of them are named above). But, as Heilbroner wrote, "…The Arrow-Debreu formulation fails to deal with the need to enumerate all such contingent markets – for example, the preference map for umbrellas next Tuesday. Without such a complete enumeration, the general equilibrium specification cannot be complete, and there can be no assurance that even minute omissions may not give rise to considerable variations in the overall ordering…." (Heilbroner, 127). In addition, Heilbroner adds, there is another conceptual key question, which concerns the circularity: The array of prices and quantities that emerges from the interaction of monads arises from the tastes and capacities of the actors. These in turn reflect their initial endowments of income and preference. Circularity enters insofar as the division of income into wages and profits, which certainly shapes the propensities of the actors, is itself the consequence of the functional division of income in the preceding period. This endless regress deprives the array of simultaneous equations of the very thing needed to establish order – namely, a knowable, objective starting point of premise (Ibid.)."

All these problems do not occur in the "Symmetric model" since the very understanding of equilibrium concept is different from the understanding of equilibrium in Arrow-Debreu model. Under the equilibrium the Arrow-Debreu model has meant such state of economy in which it may reside under certain conditions in some moment of real-time and shows what will be in this case the absolute values of equilibrium price and quantity of goods in absolute terms. At the same time, although it is clear that such conditions are completely unrealistic, and the economy itself is very abstract, but if even so we assume that these conditions can be fulfilled, it is supposed that equilibrium will be achieved in real time, which flows from the past to the future. Therefore, it is necessary to know the state from which the system begins to move toward the equilibrium point as well as all future prices, production plans, needs, accidental circumstances, etc. (Because the subjects make decisions in the present with considering the future.) For this, it is necessary to make these completely absurd assumptions that make this model unreal.

However, unlike the Arrow-Debreu model, the "Symmetric model" is not a model of a specific state in any moment of real time, which shows the real prices and quantities in absolute terms. Each price in this model is a function of all other prices and quantity of each commodity (be it a product or resource) is a function of quantities of all other goods. This model reveals the essence of economic equilibrium. It reveals only proportions between the quantities of produced, consumed and exchanged goods, and those exchange ratios between goods (i.e. relative prices), for which all that is produced is consumed and all that is consumed is produced. Therefore, all goods are exchanged with each other in such proportions that unsold goods or unsatisfied effective demand do not stay in the market. The equilibrium does not depend on absolute prices and absolute quantities of goods (products and resources). The absolute quantities of products can be arbitrary, within the limits bounded from above by quantities of primary resources (and hence, production factors) and from bottom – by minimal acceptable level of final products' consumption. But the magnitude of the absolute prices is almost unlimited if the equilibrium relative prices remain unchanged. Moreover, the model reflects the formation logic of the infinite multiple sets of mutually compatible relative prices and the relative amounts under which the system will be in equilibrium. "The symmetrical model" does not show any real state of the system at any point of real-time, but it shows only the proportions between the intra-system parameters, the internal state of a decentralized economy, with which it would be under any of the infinite number of possible variants of equilibrium, with very different absolute prices and absolute quantities. Equilibrium itself is understood as a condition toward which the system always strives from any actual state due to inherent logic of intra-system processes, but which, nevertheless, is never reached, due to the destabilizing effect of external factors.[28] Therefore, there is no need for knowledge of the starting conditions in the past or future circumstances and accidents, nor any specific amounts of goods and nominal prices. Thus, the "fullness," which Heilbroner writes about and which is necessary for finding of "fixed points" or "eigenvalues" (equilibrium prices), originally is already provided in the "Symmetric model" because of its operational closeness, which a priori encompasses all the possible prices and quantities under given constraints. As for the fact that the circularity "deprives the array of simultaneous equations of the … objective starting point of premise" (Heilbroner), from the point of view of recursive models, this fact is not a shortcoming of the model, but a significant advantage, which does not

[28] These factors can be natural conditions, social processes, new technologies, consumer preferences, propensity to risk and propensity to save, etc., the impact of which in the model is reflected in the changes of technological and consumer coefficients, rates of profit, rates of saving and interest rates.

hinder the emergence of “fixed points “and, consequently, of equilibrium prices and of general equilibrium.[29]

As an illustration, we can use the example given by Foerster. If the same operation of extracting the square root is recursively repeating, then starting with the extraction of the root from any rational number, eventually, we will inevitably get “1.” This “1” is an eigenvalue of this operation and kind of attractor or equilibrium state, which “attracts” to itself the results of recursive operations. However, if because of external circumstances (inattention, ignorance, fault of calculator, etc.) interim results of these operations deviate from their exact value, the “1” (equilibrium) will never be achieved, but the tendency to this direction will always exist.

Similarly, due to the inherent logic of recursive operations, the intersystem processes lead the decentralized economy to the equilibrium state, as to the “attractor.” Therefore, to know the initial state of the system is not necessary, because it will always move towards the equilibrium from any other state. However, due to constant influence on the system of random external factors, the general equilibrium is never achieved. And degree of deviation from equilibrium depends on the strength of the disturbing effects of random external factors. Economy always strives for equilibrium, but never reaches it.

3. Interpretation of Economic Content of the Model

1. As the quantity and price of a sold and bought product is the same magnitude it is clear that if incomes from sale of this or that product surpass the costs for its production (accordingly if the price of unit of a product surpasses its cost price), then the total quantity of sold products should also be more than that quantity which is necessary for covering of mentioned costs. There should be a source of payment of producer's profit. The quantity of sold product necessary for compensation of costs for its production is a necessary product, but other quantity from which the profit is paid - is the surplus product. But it means, also, that consumers pay for whole product more than producers have spent for its production. And someone should pay for this surplus product.

[29] “... by closing the causal chain one also appears to have gained the advantage of having gotten rid of a degree of uncertainty: no longer does one have to concern oneself with the starting conditions—as they are automatically supplied by the end conditions” (Foerster, 2003, 230).

The similar problem arises in the market of primary resources. Owners demand for their resources such prices, which allow them not only to satisfy current needs, but also to make saving. From this follows that in how many times the price of a resource is more than costs for its reproduction, in the same time the quantity of sold resource should surpass that quantity, which is necessary for covering of mentioned costs. There should be a source for covering of consumers' saving. The quantity of sold resource necessary for compensation of costs for its reproduction is a necessary resource, but other quantity from which saving is paid - is a surplus resource. And again, someone should pay for surplus resource. As to surplus resources and surplus product, surplus resources are invested into production of physical capital, and surplus products are invested into the human capital.

2. It follows from the above mentioned that proportions, in which the prices of products are distributed on costs and profit, correspond to proportions in which quantities of produced products are distributed on necessary and surplus products. But proportions, in which the prices of primary resources are distributed on consumer expenses and saving, correspond to proportions in which quantities of corresponding reproduced resources share on necessary and surplus resources.[30] But it means also that producers (buyers of primary resources) pay for all resource more than consumers (owners) have spent for its reproduction. Besides payment for a necessary resource they should pay for surplus resource. Finally, it turns out that consumers pay for final product more than producers have spent for its production, and producers pay for primary resources more than consumers have spent for their reproduction. But where is a source of payment for surplus product and surplus resource? Who is their buyer?

3. According to this model a source of payment for surplus product, from which entrepreneurial profits are formed, are entrepreneurial profits. For entrepreneurs themselves are consumers buying the final products by their incomes which are just the profits. That is, they buy a part of products produced by them from each other in the same way as all other consumers. In its essence the consumption of entrepreneur is investment in the human capital. Entrepreneurs invest earlier received profits in current consumption, in other words, this is consumption on debt, which will be paid by the future profits. But a source of payment of surplus resources from which consumers' saving are formed are themselves the saving. For saving are those free money

[30] Since a profit is generated from the value of surplus product, then surplus value is a part of the "value added." Another part of the "value added" is the value of necessary product, which corresponds to the salary, interest and rent.

resources, which through the money market are transformed into credit resources for investments into production. Just it is a source of payment for surplus resources.

That is, surplus resources are bought by entrepreneurs, but they buy them by loaned money resources generated from the saving of owners of these resources. Thus, in resource markets the saving, transformed into credit resources for investments, additionally pour in. And in the product markets the profits of all class of entrepreneurs consuming these products, additionally pour in. In addition the government buys surplus product and surplus resources. That is, they are paid from the state budget and, consequently, from the taxes that are part of the same profits and saving.

4. As we have seen, it follows from the analysis of this model that in conditions of equilibrium the cost of primary resources spent for production of given product corresponds to cost of this product spent in reproduction of primary resources. And the profit received from realization of this product corresponds to cost of this product consumed on credit (invested in consumption). On the other hand, cost of final products consumed in the process of reproduction of given resource, corresponds to cost of this resource consumed in production of final products. But the saving formed from incomes of this resource's sale corresponds to cost of this resource invested in production (consumed on credit).

To generalize the above mentioned, it follows from this model that under equilibrium conditions the total value of goods of some branch consumed in other branches, equals the total value of goods of other branches consumed in this branch, and the gross profit, saving, investment and consumption in debt equal each other. This can be termed the "Iron law" of general equilibrium. It provides formation of optimal proportions of commodity and financial flaws within the economic organism, which provide its integrity.[31] Self-regulation of market economy consists just of the ability to provide these proportions by means of market interactions of independent subjects. Finally, just this law gives clear understanding of what parts of cost of manufactured products are imputed to various production factors (Labor, Land, Capital, Entrepreneurship) by which these products are manufactured. The theory of imputation, based on law of diminishing returns, doesn't give the satisfactory answer to this question. And how production factors themselves and together with them national product are distributed between economic actors - this is already a

[31] The theory of imputation, based on the law of diminishing return, doesn't give the satisfactory answer to a question how imputation proceeds and what part of products value should be imputed to various production factors by which these products are created.

question, which depends not only on economic, but also on social and political factors.[32]

According to this model, like model of Piero Sraffa, the economy is a circular process of "production of commodities by means of commodities." In this sense this model, as well as model of P. Sraffa, is opposite to paradigm according to which the economy is the one-way process directed from "production factors" to consumer products and in which the problem of how primary resources are reproduced isn't considered (See: Sraffa, 1999, 134). However P. Sraffa considers production of production factors by means of final products in physical sense. For him there is no difference between production factors and final goods, "commodities are produced by means of commodities." For example, for him Labor is commodity produced by means of other commodities (foods, clothes etc.). But with such interpretation of manufacture of production factors it is impossible to answer a question, - what forces form a wage. Unlike early stages of capitalism, when the salary consisted of consumer goods necessary for survival of workers, today there is no direct link between consumption of goods and reproduction of Labor. Ultimately, the consequence of this approach is that from his model remains unclear how national product is divided between profits, wages, etc.

In "Symmetric model," like Walrasian model and unlike many other modern models, production factors from their services are distinctly differentiated. Producers buy not production factors but the rights of temporary use of their services. Accordingly, costs for reproduction of primary resources are reduced to costs of final products expended for reproduction of life of owners of production factors (but not of factors themselves as the legal owner, selling rights for use of factors' services. Due to such understanding, this model gives a fair idea about imputation of national income to various production factors depending on services rendered by them in its creation. Distribution of production factors between different owners (including - financial resources between entrepreneurs) in turn, stipulates the distribution of national income among the individuals.

5. The prices of final products allow to get profit, and the prices of primary resources allow to do saving. That is, the prices of final products comprise the premium over the cost of primary resources spent in their production. But the prices of primary resources comprise the premium over cost of final products consumed in the course of their reproduction. This

[32] Struggle for possession of the most scarce production factors (be it Labor, Land or Capital) always was an epicenter of conflict of political interests and defined a historical development course.

means that profit and saving compensate each other in composition of each price (be it the product or resource price). The profit in composition of product price is compensated by saving, which is a component of prices of spent resources. But saving as a part of resources' prices is compensated by profits, which are a component of prices of consumed products. The price is system magnitude. Each price is function from all other prices, they cause each other, forming math group. Therefore, from the macroeconomic point of view the equilibrium price is the price in composition of which profit and saving counterbalance each other. And in case the prices of all goods represent the equilibrium prices, then in economy as a whole the profits and saving counterbalance each other and, it means, the economy is in a condition of macroeconomic equilibrium.

6. To the extent to which producers force consumers of their products to pay excess over their expenses for consumed resources, to the same extent they are required to pay excess at purchase of these resources. And the profit is only a source of covering the additional expenses on resources. But in that case a question arises - If the profit covers only additional expenses for resources, then what is the benefit of entrepreneur? Why he runs risks if it does not give surplus? But the question is that, as a matter of fact, the profit is not any surplus, the same as saving. Only on a surface of phenomena it seems that the profit and saving are surpluses in a composition of prices of products and resources, which arise in the course of an exchange. But actually the profit is a payment for risk, which society pays to entrepreneur [33]. This is the money

[33] The neoclassical theory divides profit into normal and economic profit. But what is named a normal profit, is a payment for services of own production factors, which the subject pays to himself as he is the owner of these factors, and would pay it to another if these factors belong to another. However, in "Symmetric model" flows of incomes aren't differentiated depending on who the proprietor of factors is and to whom they are paid - to themselves or to another. Therefore, the so-called "normal profit" is decomposed on factorial incomes and is included in the structure of corresponding flows. As to economic profit, according to paradigm it doesn't exist at all in conditions of static equilibrium. The argumentation is that the profit is a payment for not insured risk, which is bound to functioning in conditions of uncertainty and presence of innovations (We do not concern problems of monopolies, as a profit source). Therefore, existence of profit is bound to dynamic economy, in which future always is indefinite. But in static economy the future is predicted, there are no innovations and uncertainty. I.e. the static economy isn't bound to risk and, hence, its compensation in the form of profit converges to zero. But it is necessary to object that the static character of model doesn't mean at all that it models economy in a statics condition. The static economy doesn't exist as that. The model, but not an economy which it models, is static. It models real, hence, dynamical economy in which both risk and uncertainty and profit always take place. The static model abstracts not from presence of risk and necessity of compensation for it, but from changes in time of economic parameters, which are caused by various factors (changes in needs, technological knowledge, investments, external economic and

expression of that part of a social product, which producers of this product demand as a payment for entrepreneurial services to society (for services of subjective production factor). However, this is a part of social production cost of product, because the product cannot be produced without entrepreneurs and hence without performing maintenance costs of their lives.

Saving is the monetary value of that part of social product, which the owners of resources have obtained from the society as a payment for the function of saving resources required for investment in production. But it is a component of costs on reproduction of these resources in the sense that saving are costs on satisfaction of one of the necessary needs in a system of consumers' needs. These are costs on insurance of future consumption, as one of the needs along with other needs. So, profit and saving are not mutually covered surpluses of products' and resources' prices over the costs of their production (reproduction). It is a payment for risk and insurance, for entrepreneurship and thrift, for enterprise and abstention, as economic functions necessary to implement the economic process.

7. Rates of profit are different in different sectors of production. But in these sectors the degrees of entrepreneurial risk caused by noneconomic (natural, social, etc.) factors are also different. Therefore, even in conditions of a perfect competition sectoral profit rates differ from each other (deviate from average profit rate). But in condition of general equilibrium sectoral profit rates should be equal to sectoral norms of surplus product. The profit rate is the price of risk. Conditions of a perfect competition mean its alignment not between various branches, but between the separate producers of the same sector. It only means that sectoral profit rates correspond to degree of entrepreneurial risk in these sectors. Entrepreneurs shift to other sectors if this correspondence is broken. The same is in the sector of resource reproduction (consumption sector). The saving rates in different "sectors" of reproduction of resources differ from each other. But the efforts of abstention in them also differ, which are necessary for creation of these saving. Efforts of abstention for creation of saving depend on size of incomes. Abstention from satisfaction of needs for necessary means of existence demands bigger subjective efforts than abstention from satisfaction of need for luxury. But the problem is not at all only in this. The problem is that difficulties of transition from one "sector" of reproduction of resources to another are caused by noneconomic (social,

natural conditions, etc., including the most entrepreneurial activity). Certainly, the model always means simplification of reality. But simplification shouldn't mean distortion of a reality and under the pretext of simplification, instead of modeled object shouldn't be put something that doesn't actually exist.

political, etc.) factors. But anyway, however the saving norms in reproduction of various resources differ in conditions of equilibrium, they are equal to the norms of investments of these resources in production.

8. We have partially simplified above the analysis to facilitate perception of article content. At the given stage it is necessary to make some specification. As it has been noted, surplus product is completely invested in a human capital, and its cost in conditions of equilibrium compensates the profits from sale of all products. But the surplus product consists not only of the products consumed by entrepreneurs and it is paid not only from profits. As it can be seen from table 6 (see: Appendix B) the surplus product consists of 3 components: 1) consumption of entrepreneurs; 2) consumers' consumption in debt; 3) changes of consumers' stocks of product. Accordingly, these expenses are paid not only from the profits invested in consumption, but also from consumers' saving, reinvested in consumption.[34] Similarly surplus resource is completely invested in a physical capital and in equilibrium conditions it corresponds by cost to volume of saving. But, in this case, the surplus resource is paid not only from saving (transformed into credits). According to this model (see: Appendix B) the surplus resource also consists of 3 components: the resources used on 1) restoration of depreciated capital, 2) net increment of capital, 3) changes of stocks of finished goods at producers. And these expenses are financed not only from consumers' saving invested in production, but also from profits, reinvested in production.[35] Thus, the part of producers' profit is invested in consumption, a part is reinvested back in production and the remaining part amounts to changes in cash accumulations in production sector. Also, the part of consumers' saving is invested in production, a part is reinvested in consumption and the remaining part amounts to changes in cash accumulations in consumption sector (See

[34] Like investments into production, investments into consumption also can be parted conditionally on "depreciation" and "net investments" into the human capital. For example, expenses for consumption of entrepreneurs, as well as expenses for maintenance of the law and order, security, public health services, social protection or government, are some kind of expenses for restoration of human capital i.e. they are the costs necessary to be carried out permanently for maintenance of existing level of human and social capital. However, this doesn't happen at accumulation, increment of human capital or any values. But net investments into the human capital are investments into the rising of a level of welfare (consumption on credit housing services, cars, home appliances etc.), in education, science, culture, public health etc. To sum up, these investments occur not only as a net increment of able-bodied population (labor and enterprise potential), but also an increment of public goods, non-material values. That is, the increase of human, social and intellectual capital, assets, which raise economic potential of a society, takes place.

[35] Depreciation charges are also reinvested of profits, which only conditionally concern expenses for production as intended for reproduction of worn out capital.

Figure 2). In state of equilibrium investment into production and into consumption should be equal, as well as reinvestments into production and consumption (See Figure 3). The diagram of distribution of gross profit and gross saving is given below.

9. The profit is formed only from the incomes from sale of surplus product, and saving - only from the sale of surplus resource. But the profit is used for investments into consumption and reinvestments into production, and saving, on the contrary, - for investments into production and reinvestments into consumption. I.e. each of them (profit and saving) is spent for payment, both for surplus product and surplus resource. But both profit and saving are the money not different from each other despite various sources of origin. Both of them together form free financial resources, which are transformed into production and consumer investments. These transformations are regulated by credit relations, in which balancing function is carried out by the interest rate. And an essence of these processes is redistribution of production and consumption opportunities in time. Demand for money for investments by D and I (see Table 6) can be satisfied not only through supply of money from money flaws P and S, but also at the expense of money assets. The significant role in supply and demand formation in money market has not only money flows P, S, I and D, but also monetary accumulation from previous saving. In the form of assets, money plays function of tank from which monetary resources replenish and leak from monetary flaws. Fluctuations of velocity of money circulation complicate the problem of interdependence of flaws P, S, I and D in the short-run. Therefore, in the short-run these flaws possess large degree of independence from each other and are interdependent through the interest rate and the money market. But in the long-run they are interdependent with all economic flaws for they carry out system functions. Accordingly, achievement of equalities P = S = I = D is provided only in a tendency, through fluctuations in time of all economic system relative to equilibrium condition, that is, through business cycles.

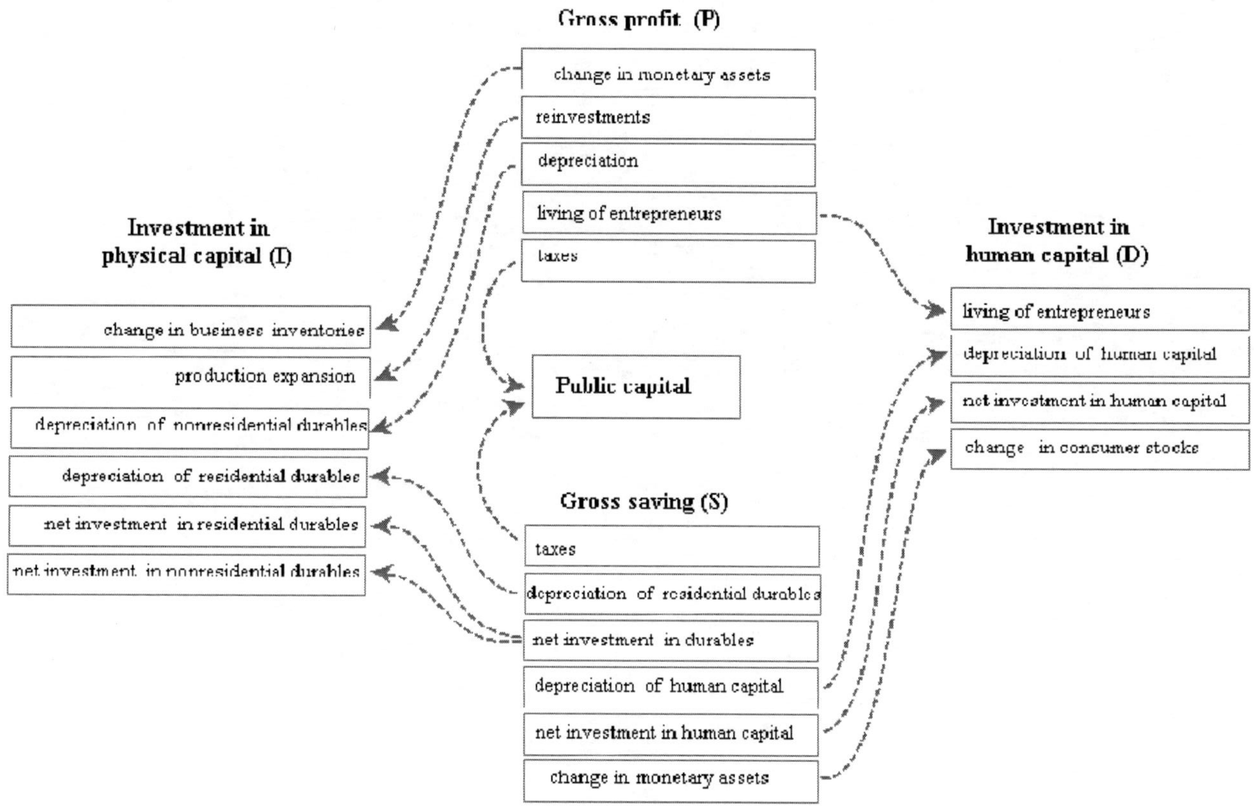

Figure 2. Scheme of allocation of gross profit and gross saving for investment in physical, human and public capital.

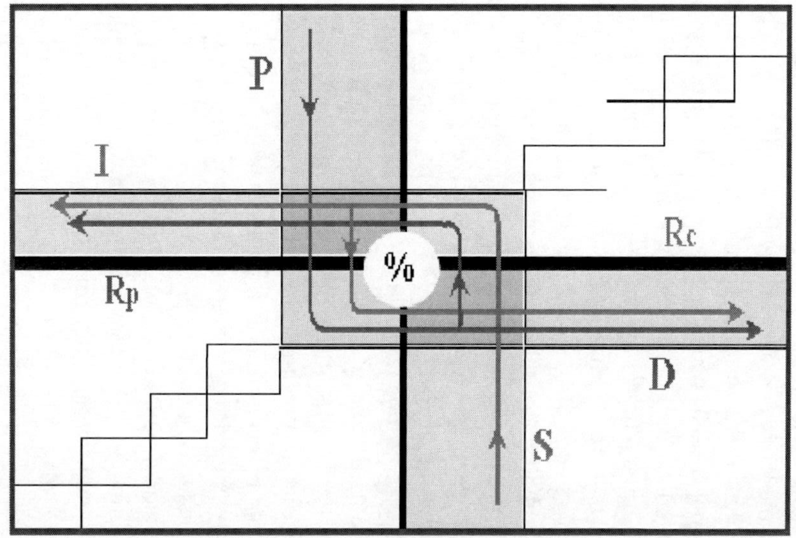

Figure 3. The scheme of allocation of gross profit and gross saving between investments and reinvestments, where P - profit, S - savings, I - investment, D - consumption in debt, Rp - reinvestment in production, Rc - reinvestment in consumption.

10. In conditions of equilibrium the outflow from producers' incomes as withdrawn profit P_n should be compensated by inflow of means in the form of credits for production investments I_g. But outflow from consumers' incomes in the form of saving S_n should be compensated by inflow of means for financing of consumption on credit D_g. That is, the condition of maintenance of demand in resources markets is $P_n = I_g$, and in product markets - is condition $S_n = D_g$. But that, as saving S_n outflows from sector 4 in conditions of equilibrium, should equal to that through the money market inflow in sector 1 as production investments I_g. But that, which in the form of withdrawn profit P_n , outflow from sector 1, should be equal to that, which in the form of consumption on credit (consumer investments) D_g inflow in sector 4. It is reflected in the model according to which production investments I and gross saving S correspond to the same element of a diagonal of sector 2. Therefore, in conditions of equilibrium of system, if to be fulfilled, equalities $P_I = A$ and $R_c = R_p$, then $I_g = S_n$. Similarly, consumer investments and gross profit correspond to the same element of a diagonal of sector 3. Therefore, $P_n = D_g$.

11. Both producers and consumers of final products have certain stocks of products, which are a component of their investments. Stocks of product at consumers are paid, but not consumed products and, as those, they are investments into consumption. Stocks of finished goods at producers are investments into production. For, stocks of finished goods at producers are not yet realized product, so it is only a potential product. For only realization of product proves that the product is recognized as a product, as social utility. But before that, it represents only embodiment of costs or the invested resources, which can bring both profit and loss in the future.

12. According to this model, market equilibrium between supply and demand is the market condition in the reviewed time interval of which as many goods are sold and bought in the market as they are produced and consumed. Clearly, quantities of goods sold and bought in some interval of time cannot be unequal. Only consumption and production, which stand behind supply and demand, can be unequal. Deviations of production from consumption are reflected on change of size of stocks of products at consumers and producers. Or, either the supernormal stocks arise or stocks are exhausted. These fluctuations of stocks are reflected on a ratio between the desire to buy and the desire to sell the goods, that is, on a ratio of supply and demand and, as consequence, on market price fluctuations[36]. In such

[36] If it is produced less than is consumed, stocks are reduced at producers, and at consumers, on the contrary - stocks increase both at those and at others. These changes of stocks are exactly in opposite way reflected in desires of consumers to buy, and desires of producers to

conditions producers want to sell and consumers want to buy at the given price different quantities of goods, or the given quantity - at the different prices. But the prices and quantities of sold and bought goods can't differ. Economic forces arise, which restore balance[37]. I.e. according to this model consumption can be both more or less than production at the expense of changes in stocks. The price deviates from equilibrium price, but it isn't equal to zero even if the excessive supply takes place[38].

13. According to this model, the pricing mechanism, which provides market self-regulation concerning which, beginning from Adam Smith to the present day, fierce debates are waging, has proved to be very simple. This is a recursive nature of pricing, i.e. the processes similar to that are inherent in many complex non-linear dynamic systems (whether physical, chemical, biological, social, cognitive, etc.). The price system is a functionally closed self-referential system. This circular organization of price formation provides self-organization of market processes. At the same time, the economic system always tends to equilibrium due to the fact that the price system seeks to equilibrium prices, which lead to matching of supply and demand and through them also to matching of consumption and production. The system also constantly deviates from the equilibrium under the influence of external and internal factors inherent in all complex systems. These deviations from

sell. That has an opposite influence on supply and demand. Growth of stocks at consumers weakens a competition between them (i.e. doesn't offer the high prices) and growth of stocks at producers – triggers a competition among sellers (to agree on the low prices). As a result - the price decreases. But reduction of stocks causes inverse processes. Market price in a surveyed time interval is only an average from many individual prices in individual transactions (commit for the same interval of time) between set of sellers and buyers, who are in competitive relations.

[37] Attempts to explain the equilibrium prices and quantity of goods through a market supply and demand, but a market supply and demand understood as a sum of individual supplies and demands, which in turn, depend on market prices, is logically a vicious circle. To understand how market equilibrium is formed, the model should reflect logic of interaction between production and consumption, but not only between supply and demand, which are derivated from them.

[38] According to Arrow-Debreu model and equilibrium models derived from it, "the goods delivered over available demand receive the zero price" (Karlin, 1964, 330). But existence of goods with zero price has no sensible explanation from the standpoints of economics. After all, excessive supply (as well as supply and demand) exists in time. If overproduction and excessive supply takes place, then supernormal stocks of those finished products will occur that can be sold in the future. Therefore these products won't have the zero price. But in case if this or that product has no demand at all and it is absolutely clear that it won't arise in the future either, then this product has no social utility at all. In that case this good is no good any more, it is no product. Such "product" becomes an embodiment of losses measured by cost of spent resources.

equilibrium and the tendency to restore it ultimately at the macro level leads to the fluctuations of economic cycle.

Operational closeness of a market economy allows a deeper penetration into pricing mechanism. To understand the anatomy of the decentralized economy is necessary to mentally abstract from the "monetary veil" and trace the logic of barter relations. From the perspective of barter a price is the exchange proportion between goods. At that, prices show in which proportions the goods are exchanged not only between individual actors, but also between the various branches. Moreover, the exchange ratios between branches, but not between individuals, are just the adequate average market prices. But individual exchange proportions, individual prices in individual bargains fluctuate around these average market prices. In the system of prices, hence, in a system of exchange proportions, the sectoral structure of economy is reflected.

The point is that the economy is differentiated integrity in itself. This means that under equilibrium conditions, each of its branches produces for other branches as many goods as to fully meet the needs of all other branches. And it itself consumes the products from all other branches to the extent necessary for such production.[39] But in this case, when all sectors produce for others and consume only what is produced by others, creates a situation, where as a result of the exchange of goods of own production, a system of prices or exchange proportions, through which all that is supplied for sale is purchased, i.e. every effective demand is satisfied. For means of payment for any demand from the sector, are the goods, which are produced in it and are offered in return. That is, under equilibrium conditions inter-sectoral proportions of production cause the proportion of inter-sectoral exchange of goods. This exchange proportion actually is a closed system of equilibrium market prices. After all, it is all the same how to express these exchange proportions as $xA = yB$ (in case of inter-sectoral exchange) or $A = y/x\ B$, or as $B = x/y\ A$ (if the price is expressed as the prices of one good, or through the A or through B). The main thing is that in conditions of differentiated integrity, when all that is produced in the system is consumed within the system and all that is produced - is consumed, in such conditions for all industries a system of exchange proportions of type $xA = yB$ is formed, which provides full clearing of markets. But the totality of all exchange proportions precisely is a system of

[39] This implies total costs necessary for the functioning of the branch, including the consumption of consumer products by the actors involved in these branches. After all, branches cannot function without actors. In the end it turns out that for the production of any goods, the goods of almost all other branches are needed.

relative prices, which actually regulates the economic processes, but which is hidden behind the "money veil" in the form of absolute (nominal) prices.

It turns out that the prices depend on the sectoral proportions. But the sectoral proportions themselves are formed as a spontaneous result of production and consumption of individual subjects, which depend on the system of market prices. Once again the circular causality turns out - the system of market prices forms the sectoral proportions, but sectoral proportions form a system of market prices. But in this case, the circular causality is not a logically "vicious circle," but is a revealed and quite understandable interaction of micro and macro- economic processes.[40]

14. As it has already been noted, the self-regulation of a market economy lies in the ability to provide the proportions between economic flows through market interaction of independent subjects. Ultimately, these flows are driven by the energy of millions of independent selfish interests of private actors, but nevertheless, this system of flows as a whole does not depend on the will of separate actors. On the contrary, it itself structures the energy of egoism, causing economic decisions of private actors and forces them to act one way or another. This very system of interdependent economic flows generates those anonymous forces, which by invisible threads bind private actors into a single economic organism and make them dependent on each other. However, they do not fully understand the logic of this interdependence and think that they are acting only in their own interests. They think that they are completely independent, because in their actions they are guided only by their needs.

However, firstly, they do not realize that their own needs are imposed on them by society and, to a great extent, are caused by the economic system. The point is that the structure of economic needs, which should correspond to the structure of production, depends on income, ability to pay and, therefore itself depends on the structure of production. That is, the structure of needs is not something given a priori, due to an arbitrary fantasy or subjective will of consumers, under which the structure of production must be tailored. The structure of needs and structure of production mutually shape each other, because we are talking only about the solvent needs, but solvency itself depends on the structure of production, and on the incomes derived from

[40] Relative to logically "vicious circle" H. von Foerster writes: "What also causes complication is that now the suspicion will be raised that the whole matter of circular causality might be mere logical mischief. We already know this from the theory of logical inference—the infamous vicious cycle: cause becomes effect and effect becomes cause. It is my intent not only to liberate the "circulus vitiosus" from its bad reputation,6 but to raise it to the honorable position of a "circulus creativus", a creative cycle." (Foerster, 2003, 230)

production (of products and resources). Thus, the structure of economic needs also is flexible and can develop on various alternative trajectories together with the sectoral structure. This provides the possibility of harmony between the needs and the possibilities of their satisfaction and, at the same time, provides the ability to keep dynamic equilibrium between production and consumption in a phase of economic recovery.

And secondly, in a market economy each individual actually has a huge range of free choice of his goals and actions (which creates illusion of his independence). But whatever action he would implement, it turns out that the results of this action are the elements of some flows from a single system of economic flows. If an action does not generate the elements of any of economic flows, such action is not at all social economic action. That is, subjects may perform social economic actions according to their will only within the capabilities provided by the system of economic flows, which ultimately are generated by these same actions and are their aggregated results.

15. The general economic equilibrium is a condition of Pareto optimality, which means that all resources are used completely and redistribution of resources can give advantage to someone, only at the expense of another's' disadvantage. Such equilibrium means that everyone who wants to work works, and works as much as he wants to work. That is, all those who work consider that 1) their work is paid adequately, and 2) at the given payment they have found optimum balance between work and rest. All entrepreneurs don't want to pass to other sectors and hence, consider that their risk is paid by adequate profit (i.e. profit rate corresponds to risk). And all savers consider that their efforts on abstention allow to create saving adequate to these efforts. That regulating role in equilibration of flaws of resources, products, and money and debt instruments is played by an interest rate. Therefore, the certain state of equilibrium corresponds to each level of interest rate.

In condition of general equilibrium in economy not only renewal occurs, but also a net increase of physical and human capital, that is, increase of economic potential occurs. By that, economic equilibrium in itself wears a germ of development and, hence, disturbance of equilibrium. The economy in the state of equilibrium pushes out itself from this state. Equilibrium is a condition of optimality, at which existing potential is completely used. And just in this condition an increment of this potential occurs. But in conditions of increased potential the existing state of economy ceases to be optimal because an unused potential appears. Accordingly, equilibrium existing before ceases to be equilibrium because the economic forces appear that are directed on use of this potential. The competition conducts a new equilibrium state and an optimality, which will be also broken owing to the internal logic of functioning of market economy.

In condition of dynamic equilibrium the optimality of economic activity means a growth of welfare in economy not at the expense of such redistribution of resources at which benefit of some is got at the expense of losses of others. In condition of dynamic equilibrium growth of welfare occurs only at the expense of a net increase of physical, human, social and intellectual capital. As a result of this, not only the quantity of available primary resources increase, but also the technological coefficients decrease that in its turn allows increase of consumer coefficients for all consumers. A unique source of economic growth is the increment of economic potential, which occurs in an equilibrium state and means optimal use of existing potential. That is, self-increase of economic potential and the economy together with it takes place.

Chapter 4

Operational Closeness of Complex Systems

1. The principle of operational closeness makes understandable how the economic system arises and functions and how order arises in it. Concerning the social systems in general, which include also the economic system, the German sociologist Niklas Luhmann writes that the operations in such systems always occur within the system. If the operation of the system takes place in the external environment, it would have lost the meaning of difference between the system and its environment. Namely, this claims the thesis of operational closeness (See: Luhmann, 2007, 95). The thesis state that the systems are operationally closed. They are entirely based on internal operations. But this does not mean that there is a return to the old theory of closed systems and hence, to the problem of entropy. The fact is that inside the theory of operational closeness it is necessary now to distinguish between the operation and causality (Ibid, 96). The principle of operational closeness has been introduced into sociology by N. Luhmann from second order cybernetics. This cybernetic approach, which was developed by the University of Illinois physicist H. von Foerster, biologists U. Maturana and F. Varela, proved to be extremely effective for the analysis of the problems of social order formation for many reasons.

> "First of all, the idea of closed circular causality has the pleasant characteristic that the cause for an effect in the present can be found in the past if one cuts the circle at one spot, and that the cause lies in the future if one does the cutting at the diametrically opposed spot. Closed circular causality, thus, bridges the gap between effective and final cause,

between motive and purpose. Secondly, by closing the causal chain one also appears to have gained the advantage of having gotten rid of a degree of uncertainty: no longer does one have to concern oneself with the starting conditions—as they are automatically supplied by the end conditions" (Foerster, 2003, 230).

Marx's reasoning, regarding the dialectical relationships between production and consumption, written as early as in the mid-19th century, is consonant with the above provisions of famous modern cyberneticians. Particularly from the following passages it becomes evident that by noting identity of production and consumption, in fact, Marx implies "circular causality," in which "cause for an effect in the present can be found in the past if one cuts the circle at one spot, and that the cause lies in the future if one does the cutting at the diametrically opposed spot." He writes:

> "Production mediates consumption; it creates the latter's material; without it, consumption would lack an object. But consumption also mediates production, in that it alone creates for the products the subject for whom they are products. The product only obtains its 'last finish' in consumption. A railway on which no trains run, hence which is not used up, not consumed, is a railway only potentially and not in reality. Without production, no consumption; but also, without consumption, no production; since production would then be purposeless."(Marx, 1955, 717) "...consumption creates the need for new production, that is it creates the ideal, internally impelling cause for production, which is its presupposition. Consumption creates the motive for production; it also creates the object which is active in production as its determinant aim. If it is clear that production offers consumption its external object, it is therefore equally clear that consumption ideally posits the object of production as an internal image, as a need, as drive and as purpose. It creates the objects of production in a still subjective form. No production without a need. But consumption reproduces the need" (Ibid, 717-718).

2. Each subsystem of social system for the normal functioning needs the products of functioning of other subsystems. Therefore, each subsystem can function normally only if all other subsystems are functioning normally, and if they provide each other with their products. Failures in the functioning of any of them will inevitably affect the functioning of other subsystems. This means that all the functions performed by the various subsystems of society are interconnected, form a closed structure and are necessary for each other and for the society as a whole. The same is true for the economic subsystem. Each of its branches and every economic action perform certain functions that are

necessary for the functioning of other branches, for performing other actions. They are interrelated functionally and form a functionally closed integrity.

According to Luhmann social system and its environment arise on the basis of recursive processes. At that the system and its environment occur simultaneously. For each system has its own environment. There is no system without external environment, as well as there is no environment without that system relative to which it is the external environment. He writes that under the "closeness" is meant not the thermodynamic isolation, but only the operational closeness, which means: the recursive condition of opportunities of own operations on the basis of the results of own operations. Such recursive relationship in which the completion of one operation is the condition of possibility for some other operation, lead to the formation of system, whose closeness is often realized thanks to complex structures; and lead to the fact that the external environment exists simultaneously with them. This result he calls the operational closeness (Luhmann, 2004, 51)[41].

3. The operational or functional closeness implies that the realization of one function is the condition for realization of another function. Ultimately, they are interconnected in such a way that they create a base of existence for each other. That is, in the system appear recursive operations appear, which are the condition of system's autonomy. At the same time it should be noted that an operational closeness reproduces itself. This is not the result of the plan, drawn up in advance by any actor. This operationally closed system reproduces itself by the fact that each economic action logically creates "its other" action. This is similar to the construction of the genetic code, where the matrix does not exist in a physical form, but in the form of the sequence of actions and functions; when for their completion they require "its other" action and function. And this chain of interconnected functions is locked in a closed system, in which all functions, one way or another, generate each other. In one of his scientific reports H. von Foerster has said:

> "You all know about the unprecedented successes of the recursive functions that are in constant use in chaos theory and indeed elsewhere. But I have the feeling that these results of chaos research can be applied by sociology only metaphorically. Why? All chaos research is concerned with functions, and functions are only relations between numbers, at best,

[41] "No system can advance into the future faster than others and thus lose the simultaneity required for contact with the environment. Even if "time," following Einstein, permitted this, the system would remain glued to its environment. The difference between system and environment can only be established simultaneously. Thus the ongoing linkage between system and environment presupposes a common chronology" (Luhmann, 2007a, 251)

> complex numbers. A function can be quadratic, one gives this function a two, out comes a four, and one gives this function a three, and out comes a nine. It operates only on numbers, but sociology doesn't work with numbers: sociology is interested in functions. And functions of functions one calls functors. A functor is, so to speak a system that is intended to coordinate one group of functions with another group, and so today I propose to develop a research program in which one is concerned with recursive functors. So that's problem number one" (Foerster, 2003, 306).

Every economic action performs a specific function, as a result of which another action is born. This new action, in turn, also performs some other function, which is derived from the previous function and, herewith, determines the function of subsequent actions, etc. Because of the circular organization of these functions the sequence of performed actions is repeated indefinitely until a circular organization of these functions exist. But these functions are performed by the actions themselves. That is, a circular organization of functions generates such a sequence of actions through which the functions performed by these actions are organized circularly and create a closed structure. In other words, functionally closed structure creates such sequence of actions of a particular type, which causes a circular organization of functions. Ultimately, it turns out that the functioning of social system depends on itself. But the dependency on itself is independency from the others, is the autonomy. A functional or an operational closeness is the basis of autonomy.

4. The definite causal processes in the empirical world correspond to the social actions. But these causal processes by themselves are not the social actions. Social actions are perceived and exist only in a teleological coordinate system, in inter-subjective space, but the causal processes - in space-time coordinate system. That is, in this case we have the perception of one and the same processes in different dimensions. But, despite the fact that the empirical processes and phenomena are generated by social actions and are interrelated by causal links, they do not constitute a single system as a separate part of spatial-temporal world. These causal processes do not stand out in the general background of encompassing causality of whole Universe. These empirical processes and phenomena are perceived as expedient actions and as a system of social actions only in the consciousness of transcendental subject and in the inter-subjective space and only thanks to the sense, which people put in them, due to their perception in a teleological context.

5. Economic values stipulate economic actions and they, in turn, stipulate certain causal processes (physical, chemical, biological, and others.), which

change reality. As a result of these empirical processes both the man himself and his environment change. But as a result of changes of empirical reality human values also change, including economic values; for value is nothing more than a teleological relation of man to the present reality, in which he sees opportunities to meet his needs. Values represent a kind of link between the real world and a system of actions.

That is, there is a relationship, on the one hand, between the economic values and a system of actions that have only phenomenological being and, on the other , between the causal processes of real world. Not only operationally closed system of values and actions influences the environment, but also the external environment influences the system. But the system of actions and the empirical world do not intersect each other. Economic values and actions (as acts of spiritual activity) cannot penetrate into the space-time world of causal processes. But also the causal processes from the world cannot penetrate into the purely subjective world of economic actions. Both these worlds influence each other, but they keep their autonomy and independence. But autonomy does not mean isolation. Empirical world itself is a system and the changes in it are made not only by the system of actions. In the environment many other processes also take place, which are casual external factors relative to the system of actions (natural processes, natural disasters, social catastrophes, devastating wars, etc.).

6. In a market economy all subjects are producers and consumers. All of them consume that is produced by other and produce what is consumed by other. Therefore, producers of this good attract to themselves consumers of this good, which simultaneously are producers of other goods. At the same time, they repel other producers of the same good, because compete with them as purchasing power of consumers is limited. That is, producers of similar goods are repelled, compete with each other, but the producers of dissimilar goods - attract, cooperate with each other. Accordingly, buyers of similar goods compete with each other (for the opportunity to buy from the most pliant seller), but buyers of dissimilar goods are attracted to each other (in order to exchange). Thus, competition and cooperation mutually generate each other and are inseparable from each other.

Due to these forces of attraction and repulsion (cooperation and competition) structuring of economic processes is accomplished, mutually coherent flow of goods and money arises. These flows form a single system (see: “Symmetric model”), which dictates to individuals the macroeconomic constraints within which they have to act as producers, consumers, buyers and sellers, investors and consumers in debt, creditors and debtors, entrepreneurs and owners. In other words, the system itself dictates the macroeconomic constraints (conditions), within which the economic agents have to perform a variety of their functions. However, these restrictions are not directly visible to the subjects. They perceive their influence and intensity only through their manifestations in the system of prices, which reflect the forces of competition and cooperation, in the form of readiness for mutually beneficial cooperation or a mutual struggle.

7. The market mechanism channelizes the uncoordinated actions of formally independent economic subjects and by that generates commodity-money flows, which are interconnected in a single closed system. Each act of interaction of subjects generates mutually opposite movement of equal by value goods and money. Accordingly, all the plurality of different actors' actions in their totality generates the counter flows of commodity and money. And since these flows exist within a single system of economic actions, in which the result of each action serves as a means for other actions, then these economic flows are locked into a single system of two closed parallel mutually opposite flows of goods and money, which are mirror-symmetric relative to each other and which balance each other. These flows of money and goods are interconnected like opposite poles of a magnet. Through the impact on money flows it is possible to affect the flow of goods and vice versa.

Economic flows shown in the "symmetric model" are formed spontaneously. They are self-organized spontaneously due to the mechanism of economic equilibrium, according to which the clash of opposite economic interests of subjects determines balancing of mutually opposite economic processes. Production is balanced by consumption, demand - by supply, buying - by selling, investments - by consumption in debt, making gross profit - by making gross saving, etc. If balance is lost the symmetry of economic flows as a single system of mutually balanced economic forces is broken. The imbalance appears which is aimed at restoring the balance. That is, because of this symmetry and mutual balancing of economic interests the sewage of all economic processes and maintaining of boundaries of fluctuations of flow happens within acceptable limits, allowing keeping the integrity of economy as a closed system of economic actions.

8. The open system always remains only partially autonomous. That is, it is independent from the external environment only in some respect, but in the other, it depends on it. The system responds only to some external factors and is neutral to all other processes in the external world (if they do not destroy the system). Therefore, not all changes in the outside world should rank as "input" signals, but only a small part of them. In this sense, the system of economic

actions is *operationally closed* and *causally open.*[42] It is closed in the sense that the causal processes of environment do not penetrate into it. And open in a sense that it is not isolated from the environment. It only responds to the important for the system changes in the environment. At the same time the system ignores all other external factors that have no value for the system. The so-called "reduction of complexity" takes place (Luhmann). That is, the system reacts selectively only to certain changes in the environment, but no causal processes from the environment penetrate into it, since they exist in different dimensions.

In this regard, Luhmann writes that complex systems with a high degree of autonomy are both independent and specifically dependent. In modern society, the economic system, the legal system or the political system are independent to a great extent. But to a great extent they are also dependent on their environment. If the economy is not prospering, then difficulties begin in politics, and if politics cannot provide certain, for example, legal guarantees, or if political intervention is too large, it creates the problems in economy. Therefore, returning to the theme of operational closeness, it is necessary to distinguish a causal dependence/independence on the one hand, and on the other, the operations performed by the system itself (See: Luhmann, 2007, 121).

The impulses, received from environment by the effects of causal processes on the system of actions, get specific continuation inside the system in accordance with the structure of intra-system functional relationships having circular organization. In other words, the system begins in its own way, specifically reacts to impacts from the environment and, accordingly, it also has a specific impact on its environment in its own way by converting "input" impulses into "output" impulses.

The operational closeness of economic system provides a constant tendency of the system to equilibrium. But the causal openness of system, the system's exposure to external influences of environment is constantly striving to disturb the equilibrium of system without which its development would be impossible. Both together, the synthesis of operational closeness and causal openness provide economic development.

---

[42] At first Luhmann divides the concept of operational closeness and causal openness and indicates that exactly the operational closeness constructs an object, system, which is capable to aware the causal relationships. Without closeness the object could not exist as a system, in any case, as a self-referential system, and would be needed the system theory of a different kind (See: Luhmann, 2007).

9. At that, the actors are not aware of this functionally closed system as integrity. They only fragmentary realize those functions and roles, which are directly related to the functions they perform. That is, they are aware of only a few fragments of the above-mentioned system; they see the function of only those subjects with which they have to directly engage in economic relations. But they do not realize that the functional relations, which their counterparties have with their counterparties, and those in turn with the other and so on, that all these relationships ultimately are closed, return to them through the same counterparties and form an operationally closed structure, which is precisely the "invisible hand" in subconsciousness of society, directing their actions and regulating economic processes.

Conclusions derived from the analysis of "Symmetric model" as well as generally structural and functional analysis of economic system, is in tune with the many ideas of French structuralists.[43] They believed that the structure was not simply a device of some object accessible to direct observation, but a set of hidden relationships, revealed by thinking in the process of moving from phenomenon to the essence. Structuralists have come to the conclusion that the concept of structure is characterized not only and not so much by a stable ratio of elements, but by the set of rules under which from one object is possible to get a second, third, etc. by rearranging the elements and certain symmetric transformations. For the cognition of structural regularities of some set of objects, it is necessary to describe their differences as the converted into each other specific variants of one and the same abstract invariant. It is necessary to abstract from the natural properties of the objects under study, and study the relationships between the elements and systemic acquired properties dependent on these relationships. Structuralists called this principle: "methodological primacy of relations over the elements in a system."

According to structuralism behind the conscious manipulation of signs, words, images, symbols can be found unconscious deep structure, hidden mechanisms of semiotic systems. Scientific objectivity of research may be provided just by the study of these structures of unconscious. These latent regularities to which men obey unconsciously, correspond to some deep layers of culture. Just they mediate the relationship of human consciousness and the

[43] Structuralism, as a scientific discipline in the humanities, was born in the 20s of XX century in linguistics and then spread to a number of areas of knowledge. But in a broader sense structuralism implies complex of scientific and philosophical ideas associated with the use of a structural method and gained the greatest expansion in the 60s in France. Representatives of structuralism are: C. Levi-Strauss, M. Foucault, J. Derrida, L. Althusser and a number of other scientists.

world. It turns out to be that consciousness and self-consciousness, which ignore this mediation by the deep unconscious structures, turn out the source of illusions about free and sovereign activity of human Ego.

To a certain extent aforesaid is true for the economic system. The "symmetrical model" reflects just this unconscious by society deep structures of social unconscious, the deepest layers of the unconscious relationships between economic actions of subjects that are not visible behind the outside chaos of economic phenomena, but that causes their actions. But as soon as these structures are cognized, the person gets the opportunity to act in accordance with these structures consciously and in their interests and not be forced to blindly obey them as to unknown and incomprehensible forces. Yet Socrates argued that the power of man over nature is based on the submission to its laws. Man's power over the market economy should be based on the same principle and then it becomes already the regulated economy. But for this you need to know its laws.

Chapter 5

BUSINESS CYCLES

1. FLUCTUATIONS OF ECONOMIC ACTIVITY

1. The market economy, as well as other complex nonlinear systems, is characterized by the cyclical nature of development. Economic theory still has no clear explanation for such behavior of the system. It is still an open question regarding endogenous or exogenous nature of these cycles.[44] However, studies increasingly show that usually complex systems, both natural and social, are subject to the principles of homeostasis, which presumably points to the endogenous nature of economic cycles and, accordingly, of periodic crises.[45] However, if the state does not take into account the specifics of functioning of economy as of a complex system, then wrong economic policies, not only can increase the frequency and depth of periodic crises, but also can provoke a deep crisis, having an exogenous nature. The cause of deep crises may also be other external factors - social

---

[44] "A serious defect of a theory and, accordingly, of models of general economic equilibrium is that ... they ignore the problem of cyclicality of economic development .... The sources of economic fluctuations, even in the real business cycle models are presumed exogenous shocks. However, after the recent crisis, questions about the nature of cycles ... again came to the fore. Therefore, theories and models which adequately reflect the economic dynamics in existing mode of production should contain endogenous factors of cycle." (Pluschevskaya, 2012, 32).

[45] Homeostatic approach to study of systems of different nature in its essence is a systemic approach to the study of complex systems. Homeostatic explores such governance mechanisms of systems, which maintain the systems' vital parameters within the acceptable limits. ".... The economy can be considered as a system in respect of which is valid the general principles of any complex systems (from chemical to biological and space), known to modern science. Such approach "fertilizes" the arsenal of economists by latest scientific methods, up to modern cybernetics and synergetics" (Kirdina, 2011, 10).

upheavals, natural disasters, etc. Such crises have already exogenous nature. Endogenous and exogenous crises have different algorithms of formation.

As it has already been noted, the economy is a complex nonlinear system, elements of which are economic actions carried out by independent private actors (individuals, households, firms) and the state.[46] Subjects realize their economic interests on the basis of appropriate economic activity. In order to understand the nature of endogenous business cycles, we must abstract from conscious corrective actions of state on the economy. On the macro-level government regulation introduces elements of reason and will into the mechanisms of spontaneous self-organization of complex nonlinear system, which makes impossible the cognition of functioning of a market system in its pure form. Therefore, we consider the process in its pure form, suggesting that the subjects of a market system are only private subjects.

On the micro level firms and households act and interact on the basis of goals set in advance, but on a macro level a system as a whole functions unconsciously. No one consciously controls and regulates the system. Fluctuations of economic activity and evolution of system is a spontaneous result of expedient actions of millions of independent subjects. The economic order here arises out of the economic chaos. The economy of firms and households themselves is based on the principles of redistribution (centralized) economy, but the economic relations between firms and households are based on the principles of a market (decentralized) economy, that is, on a contractual basis on the voluntary, equal and equivalent exchange. And since the economic relations between the millions of subjects are built on a contractual basis, on a system of contracts, and no one is forced to join those or other economic relations with other subjects, so these relationships can easily occur and be easily torn. This makes necessary and possible the self-organization of a market economy as a complex system.

The actual dynamics of economic system as a complex system is a cumulative result of external and internal factors. Therefore, the randomness of external factors together with the randomness of endogenous fluctuations stipulates a complex trajectory of economic system in the form of chaotic waves. But the complexity of the problem especially increases due to the fact

[46] In this case, the economic interests of government are the economic interests of society. But as the government can realize the economic interests of society on the basis of expedient activity, it must understand how complex systems operate. It cannot impose its arbitrary goals and ways of evolution. Government can only promote to the development of system along one of the alternative trajectories that initially are caused by the intrinsic nature of this complex system.

that waves of different levels of short-, medium- and long-term fluctuations of economic activity have superimposed on each other giving a complex shape to the trajectory of system development. Therefore, without the knowledge of the nature of a complex system from the trajectory of its movement, it is difficult to reveal the regularities. The Chaos theory (Synergetics) allows understanding of this complicated problem.

According to the theory of chaos it can be argued that economic cycles are not caused by external factors, but are endogenous. While external factors can help or hinder the change of the phases of economic cycles, accelerate or slow down the processes of expansion or a recession, but they are not the direct cause of cycles. But the internal causes and the logic of movement of economic cycle are caused by own structure of system, by immanent nature of market economy. Therefore, economic cycles are an "Eigen behavior" of economy as a complex system, which specifically reacts to external impulses of environment.

> "That until now seemed mysterious, unexplained, or even paradoxical, suddenly becomes perfectly clear. We find that the collective behavior of a plurality of separate individuals (whether the atoms, molecules, cells, animals, or humans) and, ultimately, their own destiny determined by themselves during their interaction with each other: in competition with one side, and cooperation - on the other. In this sense, synergetics can be seen as the science about collective behavior, organized and self-organized, and the behavior this is subject to the general laws. Synergetics is based on very different disciplines, including not only the physics, chemistry and biology, but also sociology and economics;" (Хакен, 2003, 24-25)

The cycles of increasing and decreasing of intensity of processes, of disintegration and integration of parts, constitute the internal law of non-linear processes; they are inherent in the very non-linear processes. Any complex structures demonstrate the inner instability to small perturbations under threat of collapse at the state of maximum development (of moment of processes' exacerbation). Thus, the fundamental principle of behavior of nonlinear systems is a periodic alternation of phases of rise and fall of activity, of increasing intensity and decay of processes of integration and disintegration.[47] All these features are characteristic of economic system.

---

[47] "Stability and instability, replacing each other, generate oscillatory regime. ... Open nonlinear systems constantly balance between chaos and order in a state of dynamic equilibrium.... ... Such oscillating process prevents the collapse of a complex structure because of its

2. We have already considered formation mechanisms of endogenous cycles when analyzing “Symmetric model.” These cycles exist in the form of fluctuations of economic activity relative to the equilibrium level or an optimal functioning of economy due to the equilibrium prices. Like in other complex systems, such fluctuations are usually neutralized at the expense of negative feedbacks that maintain the structure and close to the equilibrium state of system. But if under the influence of external factors deviation from equilibrium totally goes beyond certain limits, then the principle of positive feedback begins to operate. The processes begin to develop in a “mode of exacerbation” in a completely different scenario. The equilibrium structure is destroyed; a sharp decline in the economy begins. The system will not return to the previous equilibrium, but is quickly directed to a new equilibrium. However, a new equilibrium is formed in a deep depression, far from the economic potential of system. Volumes of commodity-money flows are drastically reduced, unemployment sharply rises and the capacities stand idle. But unlike the previous (pre-crisis) equilibrium, the system is in a state of stable equilibrium and thus to take it out of this state is very difficult. That's what has happened in all the major world crises,[48] including those during the Great Depression and the 2008 crisis. The exit from the crisis, the recovery of economic relations requires a lot of efforts and time, but in the end the unused resources and capacities once again are involved in the production and the system under dynamic equilibrium is gradually returning to the functioning at a level close to its potential. It comes back to equilibrium, but this is different equilibrium at a new level. Here the endogenous cyclical fluctuations begin again and everything is repeated.

Thus, the crisis generated by endogenous fluctuations of economic activity in the area of economic potential and the crises generated by exogenous factors, have different formation mechanisms. In the first case, the crisis is the

instability near the moment of peaking, harmonizing the pace of development of different fragments of complex structure. .... There are some universal, laws of rhythm, cycling, inherent to the living and nonliving: growth - recession - growth, etc. Only by following to "rhythms of life", to oscillatory regimes, the systems can maintain their integrity and dynamically develop." "Chaos and order - are two sides of a single dialectical essence of nature" (Meteliov, 2011, 36-40). The existence of a business cycle is necessary for self-regulation of decentralized economic system. Without such cycle an economic system would collapses. Therefore, Keynesian and monetarist methods (regulation of aggregate demand) of implementation of countercyclical policy cause the blocking of market self-regulation mechanism. In this case, the internal deformations accumulated in the economy and then at once appear as a deep and prolonged crisis (For example, the crisis of 2008).

[48] Available in view the world's major economic and financial crises of: 1857, 1873, 1907, 1914, 1929-1933, 1957, 1973-1974, 1987, 2008 – 2010.

result of "Eigen fluctuations" of the economic system relative to its equilibrium state in accordance with the "Eigen algorithm." In the second case, the crisis is the reaction of system on totally external factors, manifested as motion of the system from one equilibrium state to another. This is a movement from equilibrium that exists at a level close to the economic potential, to equilibrium which is in maximum distance from this level, in a deep and prolonged crisis.

And here a number of issues arises. How to understand the equilibrium under conditions of deep crisis if the capacity stands idle, resources are not used, and the needs of society are not satisfied? Why in conditions close to full employment equilibrium is unstable, but into the conditions of deep crisis it is stable? Why the decline occurs rapidly, but the rise is slowly? Which forces cause the system to move from one equilibrium state to another? And what is the difference between one and another equilibrium state? The Chaos theory gives quite rational and plausible answers to these questions.

2. A Few Words on History of the Problem

Neoclassics try to prove what Walras wanted, but cannot prove, namely, that there is a general equilibrium, that it is unique, stable and optimal. Indeed Arrow and Debreu have strictly mathematically proved the *existence theorem* of uniqueness of general equilibrium. But firstly, for this it is necessary to accept such a fantastic assumption that it cannot be recognized as proof. As for the stability of the equilibrium, it has not at all been proven. Moreover, a number of studies in the 50s and 60s have proved that general equilibrium is unstable. But even then majority of economists still believe that equilibrium in the real economy cannot be stable. They believe that if the economic system is not stable, it will not be able to fluctuate, and inevitably would fall apart. For example, regarding to one of the early dynamic models John Hicks wrote: "But mathematical instability in itself does not explain the fluctuations. Mathematical unstable systems do not fluctuate. They are just destroyed. Unstable state is a state in which it is usually will not remain" (Hicks, 1949). However, modern theory of chaos proves that the equilibrium of real complex system may be unstable without destroying the system. Minor changes in initial conditions eventually lead to the large and unpredictable changes in system's dynamics. This instability of dynamic systems is called "butterfly effect." For the first time the attention to this property of complex systems has been paid by A. Poincare in 1903. He writes: ... "it may happen that small changes in the initial conditions produce very large changes in the final phenomenon. Small mistakes in the first produce a huge mistake in the final. Prediction becomes impossible, and we get an unexpected phenomenon" (cited by: Crutchfield, 1986).

But scientists' interest in this phenomenon has increased particularly after 1963, when meteorologist Edward Lorenz has created a mathematical model of turbulent air flow. It is a simple model of three equations, three variables, and three constants. Despite its simplicity, this model has demonstrated an incredibly complex behavior. Minor changes in the initial values of x, y and z, initially has no tangible effect, but then sharply and unexpectedly has led to quite different results. Although the behavior of each of the variables looks arbitrary, but behind this appearance there is a beautiful structure which can be seen when all three variables are depicted on the same chart. See Figure 4.

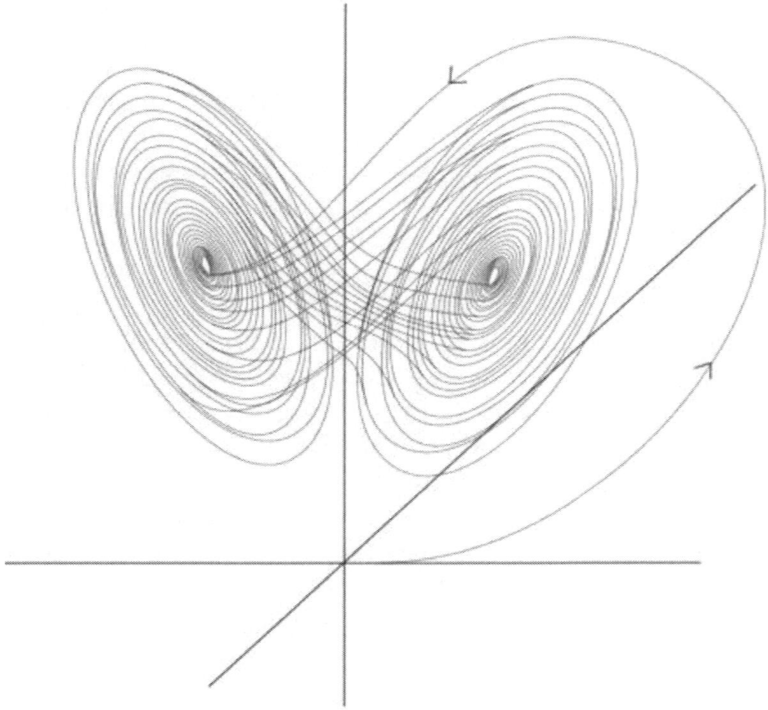

Figure 4. The set of states (or rather, points in phase space) of Lorenz' dynamic system toward which it drives in the course of time.

The analysis of Lorenz system has shown that it has not one, but three equilibriums. It is particularly important that all three equilibriums are unstable. A slight deviation from a given equilibrium makes the system very quickly move away from it. The slightest deviation from one equilibrium point leads to that the system is instantly pushed away from this equilibrium. It then comes up to equilibrium and further is pushed to the third one. It moves in its orbit around this equilibrium only for being repelled from it eventually. Finally, it approaches and then again repels from the second to the first equilibrium (See: Keen, 2011, p. 210). Such a model of behavior was in sharp contrast to point of view of Laplace, previously dominant in science (including economics), that small errors in initial indicators can only lead to a small error in predicting of the variable's future behavior.

From the point of view of mathematical technique the static analysis involves the use of mathematical models of linear, rather than differential equations. Their geometric analogues are straight lines, not lines of complex configuration, parabolas, etc. You can have hundreds of equations of straight lines and still obtain a unique solution. Linear systems cannot be chaotic. Dynamic analysis of complex systems typically involves nonlinear differential equations. But these systems can also be simple and without systems of differential equations. Chaotic behavior can occur even from the algebraic equations of second degree, that is, from the simplest nonlinear equations.

The vast majority of such systems do not have a solution. In order to see the behavior of such complex systems computer simulation is usually used. Modeling of nonlinear processes shows that the system with an unstable equilibrium is not destroyed. Such systems may exhibit a complex, cyclically repeating behavior. That is, complex systems with chaotic behavior in some sense are ordered and are subject to certain laws. This is not a random, erratic behavior, which is usually associated with the concept of chaos in ordinary discourse.

The system of nonlinear equations, used in dynamic models, does not have the solution, but it allows the modeling to determine the so-called "Attractor" - the set of possible states of a system to which it is committed with the passage of time or, in other words, the set of points at which the model can most likely be. Accordingly, although it is impossible to accurately predict the future state of model based on the available initial data, you can define the set of trajectories on which, most likely the model will move in time.

3. Economic Interpretation of Strange Behavior of Market Economy

1. Fluctuations of economic activity mean the acceleration and deceleration of economic processes. [49] What does it depend on? Economic action includes not only the transformation of some goods in others, but also the transaction, without which economic action cannot be completed. Accordingly, the economic action in itself implies transaction costs. Transaction costs mean expenses of resources, including time, arising from the conclusion of contracts, mean expenses accompanying relationships of economic agents. [50] Of course, if as a result of break off economic relations transaction costs (and especially the time losses) sharply increase, it is clear that this leads to a slowing of economic processes.

In a crisis, economic ties are broken. Although the subjects have resources, they cannot use them and cannot carry out an economic activity, since economic ties are broken. They cannot buy, because they cannot sell, respectively, cannot consume and, therefore, cannot produce. And they cannot consume because they cannot buy, but cannot buy, because they cannot sell, etc.

But nobody can understand - why? Why is all this happening? After all, no one wants this. On the contrary, they all want to produce and to consume, to sell and to buy. Some unknown force prevails over them against their will. There are producers and consumers, resources and products in the society, there are not only appropriate links between subjects, in the result of which they cannot perform economic actions. Connections are destroyed, torn. But connections are just what Synergetics studies. This question is not about the absence of objective and subjective production factors, but about the system opportunities, about the unexplained laws of functioning of complex nonlinear systems. The subjects are not able to carry out transactions and, therefore,

---

[49] Fluctuations of economic activity are usually expressed in terms of fluctuations of real GDP (i.e. of value of annual product), that is, fluctuations of ***value*** produced per unit time. But these fluctuations can also be expressed as fluctuations of ***time*** spent in production of fixed (in the starting year) magnitude of value of annual product. Economic processes sometimes are slowed down and sometimes are accelerating. In this respect Marx's remark that ultimately "any economy is reduced to economy of time" is valid.

[50] Transaction costs imply the expenditures (of time, money, labor, etc.) associated with participation in the market processes. These are the costs of gathering and processing of information, of negotiation, contracting, decision making, the costs of monitoring and legal protection of contracts execution and so on. The time losses are particularly sensitive to these processes.

cannot carry out the transformation of some commodities into others. In crisis conditions a limitation of capacity to implement the transactions becomes an obstacle; transaction costs increase sharply and especially the cost of time increases. And in the optimality conditions these costs are minimal. In addition, the search for contractors associated with risk of opportunistic behavior: possible fraud, dishonest behavior of partner, etc.[51] That is, in addition to objective costs (time, money, and resources) transaction costs include a large element of spiritual efforts, subjective costs. These subjective transaction costs increase sharply in crises conditions. Thus, transaction costs are expenditures on creation of economic ties between the subjects, on creation of economic order, i.e. expenditures for reducing of entropy in economic system. Under equilibrium conditions the transaction costs are minimal.

> "In the neo-institutionalism any act of exchange is understood as an exchange by the "bundles of property rights." The channel, through which they are transmitted, is the contract. It fixes just powers and the conditions under which they are to be transferred. This is another key term of the new institutional theory. Interest of economists to the actually existing contracts also have prompted the works of R. Coase (in general equilibrium models present only perfect contracts in which all possible future events were taken into account in advance). ... According to the neo-institutional approach, the choice of the contract is always dictated by the reasons of transaction costs' economy" (Avtonomov, 2002, 662). "The Coase theorem states: "If property rights are clearly defined and transaction costs are zero, then the allocation of resources (production structure) will remain unchanged and effective regardless of changes in the distribution of property rights." In such a way the paradoxical state is put forward: when absence of transactions costs the structure of production remains the same regardless of who owns what resources" (Ibid, 665).

The Ronald Coase's conclusion is confirmed in a proposed "Symmetric model" of equilibrium. There are no transaction costs in this model since this is the optimal model, the ideal case. At the same time in this model the structure of production does not depend on who owns what resources, for this

[51] This risk largely depends on social capital, on trust in society, on social norms and decency of society as a whole. "Social capital is a definite potential of a society or a part thereof, arising as a result of the presence of trust among its members. ... Social capital differs from other forms of human capital that usually is created and transmitted through cultural mechanisms - such as religion, traditions and customs. "(Fukuyama, 2004, 52)."... Distrust, widespread in society, imposes on all of its economic activity something like an additional fee, which does not have to pay the society with a high level of trust" (Ibid, p 55).

model only reflects the ongoing economic functions and ignores the distribution of functions between the subjects.

2. In the economic system, all subjects are interrelated. Production and consumption of commodities of each subject depends on the production and consumption of commodities of all other subjects. This relationship involves not only the qualitative and quantitative determination of commodities, but also coordination between these processes in time. In certain limits divergences of rates of production and consumption of various subjects are tempered by the existence of commodity stocks, by finding alternative contractors, etc. But if for whatever external, accidental causes are, the acceleration or deceleration of economic activities encompasses some critical number of interrelated subjects, a cumulative process will begin there, which will tighten a majority of other subjects too. The expansion or recession will begin, which will continue by inertia until achieving the turning points - a peak or a bottom. This explains the general cause of oscillatory motions in conditions of universal interconnection of system components. That is, a fact of universal interconnection of market agents by itself determines a coherent, ordered behavior, the cause of coordinated growth or decline of their economic activity, the total wave of acceleration and deceleration of economic processes in the system as a whole. The very integrity of the economy as a system of economic actions is caused by just this general relationship between economic agents, each of which by their actions produce commodities for others by means of consumption of commodities produced by others.

> "It is different with the collective behavior. Exactly it is the subject of research in synergetics. When we shall henceforth to talk about the collective behavior, we will mean by that such behavior in which people act as if they have conspired among themselves" (Haken, 2003, 165). "Every system is subject to external conditions. These conditions are described in the form of so-called control parameters. If the control parameters are changed, the system can constantly adapt to new conditions. ... Under quite certain values the control parameters sharply change the behavior of the system. This new behavior can be described - again surprisingly - by the few variables, the so-called order parameters. ... All order parameters perform some function: they determine the behavior of separate parts, just as the invisible player in a puppet theatre controls the behavior of the dolls. In synergetics this is the principle of subordination. ... Initially the separate parts define the order parameters by their behavior. From the standpoint of synergetics, we are dealing here with the circular causality. The order parameters determine the behavior of parts and vice versa, through their collective behavior parts determine

> the behavior of order parameters" (Haken, http://bookfi.org/g/Haken). "Here we are again confronted with a kind of relationship between individuals and the ordered structure. The structure subordinates to itself the individuals; however converse is also true: precisely the individual support the existence of the structure" (Haken, 2003, 189).

Something similar is happening in economy. For example, the dominant social expectations of economic expansion or recession, inflation or deflation, subdue personal views and individuals' actions and spread further and further. In this way these expectations support their own existence. In terms of Haken expectations prevailing in society play the role of "order parameter."

3. Exogenous crisis is a state of stable equilibrium, from which begins the ascent with preservation of dynamic equilibrium. As the economy approaches to its potential the equilibrium becomes less stable, and reaching a level of full employment the economy is in a state of unstable equilibrium. Here the boundaries of stability are narrow. By breaking these boundaries the economy enters into recession. The sharp downturn caused by the totally effecting external factors is a catastrophe in which an economic system qualitatively changes its properties, there arise disparities in a structure, the system temporarily loses integrity (there breaks the unity of the parts shown in the "Symmetric model"). This is a disorganization of system as a result of destruction of equilibrium structure and the rapid decline by a chain reaction until the lowest point of collapse. The process ends with a deep and prolonged crisis. At the bottom the equilibrium is gradually restored in sharply limited scale of mutually agreed economic flows.[52] Then again begins a gradual rise with keeping of dynamic equilibrium. That is, the system moves from one state of equilibrium at full employment, to another - under conditions of deep crisis. Based on the analysis of behavior of complex systems, Haken concludes:

> "Even our previous reasoning and observations contradict to that traditional theory of free market economy, which dates back to the times of Adam Smith. He proceeded from the fact that in free competition is always set one - and perhaps even the only - state of equilibrium. However, we have already considered the opposite example: the case of the emergence of not one but two possible stable states. At that for economy in general is not simple to "jump" from one stable state to

[52] Otherwise, the decline can be represented as a sharp deceleration of processes caused by rupture of former and chaotic searching for new connections, and the bottom – as restoration of equilibrium in conditions of significant slowing of economic flows.

another because the process often becomes possible only thanks to some collective actions. In reality the economic behavior is much more complicated. Suppose the economy can constantly move from one stable state to another like a pendulum. At that a full employment periodically is replaced by a partial unemployment" (Haken, 2003, 182). "In these cases the most important role is played by a collective behavior. On the basis of this behavior there may occur such phenomena that decisively diverge from a classical economic theory in the spirit of Adam Smith and his postulate of economic equilibrium" (Ibid, 188).

4. The deep decline in economic activity, periodically generated by exogenous factors, has its own characteristics quite understandable from the view point of the theory of complex systems. As has been noted, in conditions of full use of resources, in an optimal operation regime, when the economic system is in equilibrium, the system is unstable, but under conditions of deep crisis in a mode of non-optimal operation regime, when the system is also in equilibrium, the system is stable. This is due to the fact that in conditions of full employment an economic system becomes hard and brittle. Decreased flexibility and fragility of system is related to the fact that as we approach the economic potential the free resources stay less and less. But in conditions of exhaustion of free resources in a state of equilibrium, when all sectors operate at the limit and in full coherence and harmony with each other, the slightest underproduction or overproduction in one or another branch of the same becomes the reason of overproduction or underproduction of related branches that takes out the system from equilibrium. In the context of global interdependence of branches this disorder triggers a chain reaction, which is difficult to stop. But in times of crisis and availability of unused resources such problem, of course, does not arise.

During the expansion, the involvement of resources into the economic processes is possible only in the mode of mutual coordination, only in compliance with proportions between economic flows. Therefore, their involvement occurs in a gradually orderly manner, in coordination with each other. This requires time. But when recession takes place, the breaking of ties does not require much time, occurs quickly and by a chain reaction spreads throughout the system. Therefore, the decline occurs quickly, but recovery occurs slowly. In conditions of full employment, when all the resources are involved in economic processes and all the actions of the subjects are arranged and organized in mutually coordinated economic flows, the *entropy* of economic system is minimal. At the bottom, in conditions of crisis, when the stable economic ties are broken and the subjects are chaotically looking for potential partners in conditions of high risk opportunistic behavior, the *entropy* is maximal.

Periodically appearing deep and prolonged exogenous crisis and subsequent economic growth generate waves of economic activity of a higher level than the endogenous cyclical fluctuations. “Eigen algorithms” of system behavior in one and the other case is different. In the first case, there takes place a gradual approximation of system to an economic potential in a regime of dynamic equilibrium and then a sharp rebound from it into a deep depression. Destruction of old and formation of a new equilibrium structure of economic flows takes place. Out of the depression the system with a new structure gradually again approaches its potential in the regime of dynamic equilibrium. And everything is repeated. As for endogenous cyclical fluctuations at the peak of the long waves (i.e. waves generated by exogenous factors), towards them these fluctuations appear as random fluctuations regarding the unstable peak equilibrium. That is, at the peak, in an equilibrium state, there exists a stability threshold and as soon as the system oversteps it, the system will roll into a deep crisis (the Great Depression, 2008 crisis, etc.).

5. One of the founders of Chaos theory Prigogine wrote: “In the case of an isolated system the equilibrium acts as an attracting set, or of “attractor” of non-equilibrium states” (Prigogine, 1986, 88). Why does an economic system move to an equilibrium state, as to the attractor, in which there are no losses and the system reaches an optimal state? This is because each subject seeks to avoid losses and is committed to an optimal state. That is, there is a complete coincidence of interests of all subjects from the actions of which the system is made up. Moreover, this state can only be achieved under equilibrium conditions.

> “An attractor is a steady state (structure) of the system, which as though “attracts” (from the Latin: *attrehere* - attract) to itself all the set of “trajectories” of system defined by different initial conditions (if system falls into the cone or sphere of attractor, then it inevitably evolves to this steady state / structure). While in most papers on problems of self-regulation under the attractor is understood an image of a this relatively stable state in a phase space, in this paper as attractors are called the real structures in open nonlinear environments, to which go the evolutionary processes in these environments as a result of damping of intermediate, transitional processes. Underlining this we often use an integral formation “structure-attractors” (Kniazeva, http://lib.icr.su/node/1247).

The subject can increase its property either by creating values or through redistribution. To create value is possible only in conditions of cooperation with other actors. Therefore, everyone is looking for mutually beneficial cooperation with other subjects and here the interests of all actors are the same. But the actors can get unilateral benefit also due to redistribution. Here begins the divergence of interests of partners. The competition between the subjects comes into force. In this competition, they restrict each other from encroachment on their interests. Under conditions of economic equilibrium and the balance of interests of all subjects, the maximum benefit of each of them is restricted by the limit, after which a further increasing of benefits is associated with losses of another subject. This is a condition of Pareto optimality. That is, the system is functioning optimally in conditions of Pareto optimum, which is achieved under conditions of equilibrium, which is characterized by a balance between the opposite forces of cooperation and competition. The "Symmetric model" is just such a perfect model of economic equilibrium, in which the economy achieves the optimal functioning due to the balance of opposing interests.[53]

6. The crisis is the purification from the archaic and unsustainable and verification for strength of everything new and viable, of all that is necessary for the progress and evolution. On a wave of expansion and movement from depression to a new peak of development in economic system there arise the new functional connections, structures, open up new markets, are born and satisfied new needs, introduced new technologies, etc. However, some of them are viable, others - no, some are necessary for the further development of society and economy, others - are accidental, some are progressive, others - regressive. But during recessions, all that is unsustainable and hinders development, dies, is eliminated forever, all that is short-lived and accidental. But all that is progressive, sustainable and necessary - is maintained. That is, a grand total of wave-like motion of a system is the preservation of all useful and progressive, in the result of which the development of system takes place. Therefore, the system fluctuations take place relative to the long-term trend of system development. But that trend is only implied and the actual trajectory of system has a zigzag shape in which each successive peak is higher than the previous peak, and each bottom is above the previous one. This process is

[53] "Symmetric structures are asymptotes, attractors, goals of self-organization processes. It is found in particular that in the environment can be developed the structures of different degrees of complexity and of different types of symmetry, ... At that the symmetry is a condition of meta-stable self-renewal of complex structure ..." (Kniazeva, http:// lib.icr.su/node/1247).

similar to Darwin's natural selection. For when something new is created, nobody knows in advance how much it is necessary and viable. Only time shows this. This method of evolution by "trial and error" is the only way of development in conditions of absence of conscious development of goals of system. Here the system is moving towards a certain goal without any centralized intervention of someone's reason and will and is an unintended result of interaction of millions of rational actors, purposefully pursuing only their own private self-interests, not taking care of purposes of a system as a whole. As progress is made, the government begins to increasingly realize the goals of system and begins to centrally affect the system itself in public interests, based on the knowledge of the laws of its development.

7. In the conclusion of this chapter, we note that the fluctuation in general implies movement from one extreme to another, opposite extreme. And the presence of the opposite extremes in itself implies the existence of an equilibrium state relative to which can only be a deviation and, therefore, only in this case it may make sense to talk about the fluctuation itself. In economic reality we see cyclical fluctuations of economic activity at different levels. But we do not see an equilibrium state, level, path or long-term trend, regarding to which the fluctuations occur. We only mean their existence, because fluctuations may be observed only in the background of the implied equilibrium. Equilibrium is the "blind spot." It is unobservable. But all that is observable is observable due to the "blind spot." If there were no equilibrium, changes of economic activity would not be perceived as fluctuations, but as a chaotic, disordered, random motion and no regularity in their motion would be possible to detect.

Chapter 6

ENIGMA OF ADAM SMITH

1. ESSENCE OF THE PROBLEM

According to Smith the value of each individual product is equal to the sum of incomes consisting of wage, profit and rent. He has not acknowledged the capital expenditures as the fourth component of price because they match the value of previously created products of labor, which in turn is divided into the same three elements as the final product is. Smith's position is quite reasonable: the inclusion of capital expenditures into the price of all goods would lead to the fact that one and the same product would enter the yearly product of society repeatedly. By this approach, Smith avoids double counting in a measurement of annual product. But Smith argues that if the value of each individual commodity falls into incomes, this should apply to the whole mass of commodities, composing the annual product of each country. Therefore, the value of national product should also be equal to the sum of incomes consisting of wage, profit and rent. But the core of the problem is that the part of annual product produced in the country is the capital goods required to replace depreciated capital. For the society their value is the costs required for production of annual product. It turns out that the cost of each product individually consists only of incomes, but the value of entire national product, which consists of these products, in addition to incomes, includes also the value of depreciated capital. But after all within the prices of individual products the value of depreciated capital has already been decomposed into incomes. Why does it occur again in the national product? This enigma remains enigma and generates a number of problems. The value of final product turns out to be greater than the amount of incomes. It turns out that the aggregate supply is greater than the aggregate demand; that the entire product cannot be sold inside the country. But economic reproduction is possible only under the condition that all goods will be sold, all the means of production and consumption goods - recovered. Consequently, the crises are inevitable, etc.

A. Smith cuts down this “Gordian knot” and just gets rid of the problem by introduction of concepts of “gross” and “net” products. But from a purely theoretical standpoint - this is incorrect. Here clearly exists ambiguity, which remains so up to this day. This is just reflected not only in theory, but also in the System of National Accounts. Here's what the authors writes in the SNA 2008:

> 2.141 In principle, the concept of value added should exclude the allowance for consumption of fixed capital. The latter, in effect, is not newly created value, but a reduction in the value of previously created fixed assets when they are used up in the production process. Thus, theoretically, value added is a net concept. This conclusion applies to domestic product as well; theoretically, domestic product should be a net concept. Net domestic product (NDP) is obtained by deducting the consumption of fixed capital from GDP.
>
> 2.142 However, gross measures of product and income are commonly used for various reasons. ... So GDP is broadly used even if it is, on a conceptual basis, economically inferior to NDP.
>
> 2.144 The remarks above about the conceptual relevance of the net concept in case of product apply even more strongly to national income (SNA 2008, p. 34).

So, division of national product and national income into “gross” and “net” cannot be considered as a solution. On the contrary, such division essentially hides the real problem, creates illusion of its solution and thus conserves the problem. Smith deviates from solving of the problem and leaves this enigma unsolved. Since the days of Smith a large number of economic works is devoted to this problem, but it still remains unsolved (See: Marx, 1992; Luxemburg, 1968; Kalecki, 1968; Moseley, 1998; Trigg, 2006). And it cannot be solved as long as economic theory reaches a clear understanding of how the economic reproduction is performed.

2. Model of Economic Reproduction

1. In essence, the theory of reproduction also is a theory of equilibrium. But it is the theory of equilibrium not between the supply and demand, but

between production and consumption. If all economic processes are considered only at the market level and not at the production and consumption level, the search for economic equilibrium loses a "pivot" and the connection with fundamental economic laws, which govern the functioning of economic organism as a whole. Reproduction theory explores the objective economic laws, ensuring the possibility of equilibrium, at a deeper level of economic performance. At the division of labor, various branches of economy should bring into accordance their outputs with one another and exchange their products between one another. At that, not all these proportions of production, distribution, exchange and consumption are equally important for the normal functioning of the economy.[54] But there are some "necessary" proportions between departments of economy (i.e. the groups of economic branches), in case of violation of which, the integrity of economic organism will be violated. The deficits and surpluses will arise; producers can't sell the product, obtain necessary resources; production will reduce or stop. These "necessary" proportions are caused by objective economic laws and are necessary for maintaining a macroeconomic equilibrium. If implemented, the economy as integrity consists only of its necessary parts and consists of nothing random and unnecessary. All of the resources are used, all products sold, all solvent needs met. And what is most important, as a result of this process all the necessary *preconditions* for continuation of economic process in the previous regime of dynamic equilibrium are reproduced. It means that the theory of reproduction implies the reproduction not only of final products, but also of primary resources as well as of solvent needs, which drive the entire economy. Therefore, the theory of economic reproduction is impossible without understanding of reproduction process of economic subject as a consumer, entrepreneur, owner, as a generator of economic needs and incentives.[55]

2. Below is shown a diagram of formation and distribution of economic flows in condition of a simple economic reproduction.[56] We consider a closed economic system. Here is represented the matrix consisting of four quadrants:

---

[54] Many of the products and resources are interchangeable, so discrepancy between production and consumption of some goods, within certain limits, can be compensated by opposite deviations in production and consumption of other goods, so that macroeconomic equilibrium will not be disturbed.

[55] At that, these proportions are necessary for harmonic operation not only of market economy, but of any economic system, whether natural, market or regulated economy. Although in all systems the forces, which ensure the preservation of these proportions, are the economic interests of interacting agents, but the specific mechanisms of restoration of "necessary" proportions in the case of deviations from them, differ from each other.

[56] For more details this diagram is considered in Leiashvily P. (2012). Economic Activity: Teleological Analisys. NY, Nova Publisher Inc., p. 121.

I - production sector, II - market of final products, III - market of primary resources, IV - consumption sector (reproduction of primary resources). The rows of matrix represent different sectors of reproduction of products, resources and capital goods, and the columns show their allocation and consumption in various sectors. For example, sector 1 simultaneously shows the transformation process of primary products into final products and the imputation process of final products to primary resources. The elements of this sector simultaneously reflect the value of services through which the products are produced and the value of those parts of final product, by which these services are remunerated. Therefore, each element simultaneously shows the value expressed in final products as well as the value expressed in amount of income, received by some agent of production. I.e. it shows the imputation of final products to production factors according to their contribution to the production process.

During the transformation of primary resources into final products the surplus product is created. The total value of final products (i.e. necessary plus surplus products) is Domestic Product (DP), which is shown in Sector 2. At the same time, the value of this final product equals incomes that have been created during its production. Sector 3 shows the allocation of value of final product between primary resources, entrepreneurial income and taxes, which add up to National Income (NI). There are empty cells in the diagonals of sectors 2 and 3. In sector 2 this cell indicates that in composition of DP the capital goods are not considered, by which worn capital has been replaced, because they are not intended for final consumption and are not a final product. And in Sector 3 an empty cell indicates that in composition of NI are ignored the depreciation allowances from profits are ignored, for they are not the primary income, although they are a part of gross profit.

In sector 1 red arrows show the exchanged parts of final products of different departments of economy. According to this model, in conditions of simple reproduction the whole product of department, producing nonresidential durables, excluding depreciation of this department, completely replaces the worn-out capital in all other departments of production sector (red arrows). As to depreciation of departments, producing nonresidential durables, the branches, belonging to this department, without residual are sharing that part of their surplus product, which reflects the magnitude of depreciation in these branches.

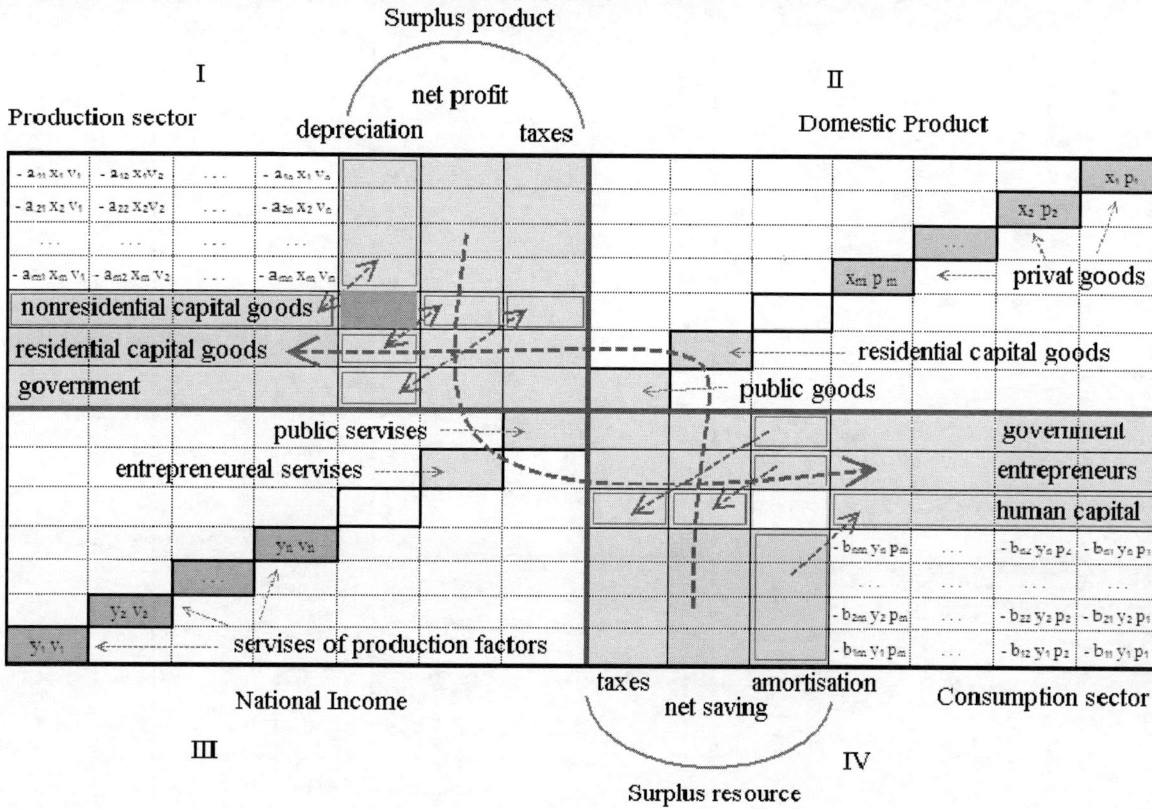

Figure 5. “Symmetric matrix” of economic flows in closed decentralized economy.

The columns of Sector 4 show the distribution of final product for reproduction of primary resources, human capital, entrepreneurial and public services.

As a result of final products' consumption not only a necessary resource is reproduced, but also a surplus (saved) resource. The red arrows in Sector 4 show the direction of income reallocation, necessary for reproduction of human capital.

As we see, both production and consumption sectors have net income (profit and saving), which is used for investment in physical, human and public capital.

3. *A numerical example.* For a more concrete analysis of conditions of simple reproduction we take conditional values of key parameters. See Figure 6.

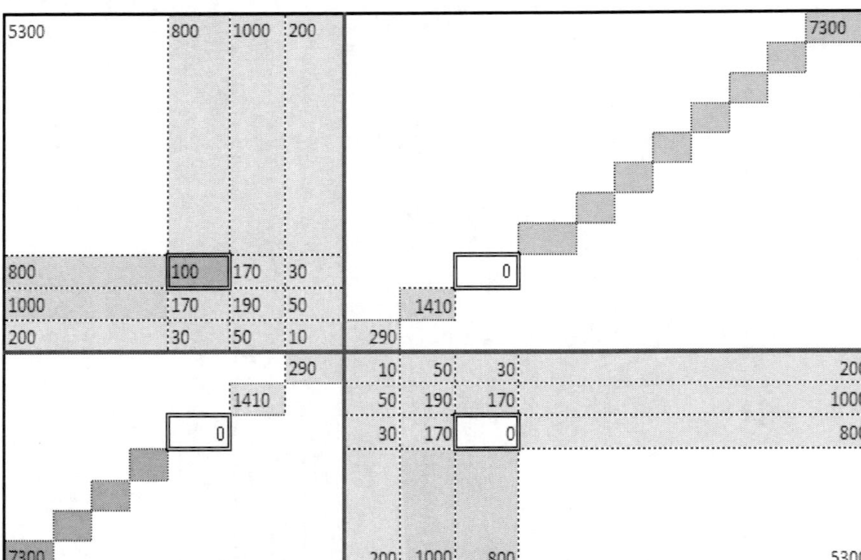

Figure 6. The “Symmetric matrix” of economic flows (numerical example).

We write out the values of parameters in a compact form, as is shown in Figure 7.

	A	B	C	D					DP 9000
I	5300 a	800 b	1000 c	200 d				7300	
II	800 a	100 b	170 c	30 d			0		
III	1000 a	170 b	190 c	50 d		1410			
IV	200 a	30 b	50 c	10 d	290				
				290	10 e	50 f	30 g	200 h	V
			1410		50 e	190 f	170 g	1000 h	VI
		0			30 e	170 f	0 g	800 h	VII
	7300				200 e	1000 f	800 g	5300 h	VIII
NI 9000					E	F	G	H	

Figure 7. The matrix of numerical values of economic flows.

Indications of lines:

Reproduction of products (resource consumption):

I - reproduction of consumer products;

II - reproduction of nonresidential durables;

III - reproduction of residential durables;

IV - reproduction of public goods.

Reproduction of resources (consumption of products):

V - reproduction of public services;

VI - reproduction of entrepreneurial services;

VII - reproduction of human capital;

VIII - reproduction of primary resources - services of Labor, Capital, and Land

Indicate the columns:

Productive consumption (reproduction cost of final product):

A - consumption of services of production factors (of Labor, Capital and Land).

B - consumption of nonresidential durables (depreciation);

C - consumption of entrepreneurial services;

D - consumption of public services.

Consumption as such (reproduction cost of primary resources)

E - consumption of public goods;

F - consumption of residential durables (amortization);

G - incomes of production factors in the process of reproduction of nonresidential durables;

H - consumption of consumer goods.

To each element of diagonal corresponds row and column. As we see, diagonals of sectors 2 and 3 are symmetrical to each other, as well as sectors 1 and 4 (except disparity of cells II B and VII G, the cause of which will become clearer below). The symmetry is also found in sectors 1 and 4.

The simple reproduction assumes that the following conditions are met:

1) I = A = VIII = H. This means that reproduction of consumer products and primary resources (services of labor, land and capital) equals to their consumption.
2) II = B = (G -100) = (VII - 100). In conditions of simple reproduction as many nonresidential durables (II) are reproduced, as are consumed (B). Value of products consumed in debt (VII) is equal to the value of incomes received during production of nonresidential durables (G).
3) III = C = VI = F. Reproduction of residential durables (III) equals to their depreciation (F), and the personal consumption of entrepreneurs (VI) is equal to the value of entrepreneurial services[57] (C).
4) IV = D = V = E. The public goods and services are produced as many as are consumed.

In simple reproduction the changes in production and consumption of stocks and the changes of monetary assets of producers and consumers equal to zero. Also, a net increase of all kinds of capital is absent. There is only a compensation of consumed capital. Therefore, the value of product of department II is equal to wearing of nonresidential durables in the production sector (B):

$$II\ (800\ a + 100\ b + 170\ c + 30\ d) = B\ (800\ b + 100\ b + 170\ b + 30\ b) = 1100; \qquad (1)$$

The elements of rows of matrix indicate from what components the value of that or another final product is composed. If the value of these components is expressed through the share of final product, we find that at compensating

[57] i.e. the value of goods, by which society paid for entrepreneurial services .

the worn capital the different fractions of product of department II are exchanged for different fractions of surplus product of departments I, III and IV. Thus, the following proportions of the value of exchanged products are kept:

800 IIa = 800 Ib; (2)
100 IIb - remains in department II;
170 IIc = 170 IIIb; (3)
30 IId = 30 IVb; (4)

Although produced nonresidential durables are fully exchanged for the products of other producers and do not enter into the consumption sector, but the products, for which they are exchanged, are intended for consumption. Therefore, in consumption sector is reflected the redistribution of only residential goods (durables and nondurables). Accordingly, parallel with transposition of lines II into column B in the first quadrant of matrix (as a result of replacing the depreciated capital), column G is transposed into the line VII in consumption sector. Column G represents that part of owners' incomes (800 VIIIg), entrepreneurs (170 VIg) and government (30 Vg), which they receive as payment for their services in production of nonresidential durables. This part of incomes corresponds to the value of final products spent in restoration of human capital. In the end, we find that the final product produced in departments I (7300), III (1410) and IV (290) is completely consumed by all consumers (owners, entrepreneurs and government). Also, all services, provided by the owners (7300), entrepreneurs (1410) and government (290), are completely consumed by all producers. And all that is produced in department II (1100) is used by all producers in departments I, II, III and IV. At that the following conditions are satisfied: NP (9000) = NI (9000). That is, the system is in equilibrium and all necessary conditions of simple reproduction are met.

According to the earlier given definition, the capital, produced to replace the worn capital, is intermediate product. Because this product is not sold beyond production sector, it is not intended for final consumption of society and is not the final product of society.[58] So it is not included in composition of

---

[58] In SNA 2008 is pointed "Intermediate consumption does not cover the progressive wear and tear of fixed capital. The latter is recorded as a separate transaction (consumption of fixed capital)" (SNA 2008, p. 24). But this is wrong, because consumption of fixed capital just is "the using up of goods and services when producing this output (intermediate consumption)." But it should be clarified that this intermediate consumption is consumption

DP. On the other hand, since the depreciation allowances do not go beyond production sector either,[59] then, in accordance with definition given above, they are not the primary incomes. Therefore, depreciation in composition of gross profit is not a part of NI.

4. According to this reproduction pattern, in indicator GDP, in that form in which it is calculated in SNA, the value of consumed capital is calculated twice: Firstly, as the value of capital goods, by which depreciated capital was replaced and secondly, in composition of value added of all other goods. When calculating according to the value added method, the indicator DP contains the value of depreciation fund, as a part of gross profit and, therefore, as a part of the value added. Accordingly, the value of those capital goods should not be additionally introduced into the indicator DP, which is paid from this fund. Even more, these goods do not represent the final product. GDP indicator distorts the real value of final product of society and overstates it by the amount of consumed capital. The true indicator of final product of society is an indicator that in SNA is calculated as NDP. However, it should be simply named Domestic Product and opt out of division of this index in “gross” and “net.” In economic sense, there exists only one parameter of Domestic Product, which is equal to National Income.[60]

5. Incomes, received in reproduction of depreciated nonresidential durables, are paid from the depreciation fund, therefore, from the profit of all other producers. In natural form these incomes consist of surplus product of all other branches producing residential goods (durables and nondurables). These are those final products, which society sacrifices to those, who were engaged in reproduction of worn-out capital. Value of these products has a dual nature. It is perceived as expenditure for producers of consumer goods, and - as income for those, who reproduces worn out capital. But from the viewpoint of society, this is only a redistribution of value added between producers of different industries. Accordingly, the cost of depreciation is taken into account in DP in the form of depreciation fund, and in NI in the form of income of those producers, who produce the capital goods for recovering the depreciated capital. And as incomes of mentioned producers, ultimately are formed from depreciation funds, the indicators of DP and NI are equal. Therefore, it appears

in debt. So the production of capital goods for replacing depreciated capital is the compensation of this consumption in debt by equivalent investments. Accordingly, in contrast to the net investment, the capital goods, replacing depreciated capital, are not the final product of society.

[59] They are transformed into the incomes of agents producing capital goods for replacement of worn-out capital and only as their incomes are derived into the consumption sector.

[60] Accordingly, no "problem of realization" in the economic theory arises.

that the DP and NI indicators, calculated by the value added method, simultaneously take into account also a consumed capital without violating the very principle of formation of these indicators.

6. As for the depreciation fund of the department itself, which produces nonresidential capital goods, it does not need special accounting in NI or DP. For the branches, belonging to this department, produce and sell to each other capital goods for replacing worn-out capital. It's like an exchange by parts of surplus products between the branches of this department. So, this part of surplus product does not go beyond this department, does not present a demand for the products of other departments and itself does not become the object of demand of other departments of economy. That is, this is an intermediate product produced and consumed completely within the same department.

7. We have studied the conditions of simple economic reproduction. But from the matrix it is easy to understand how to maintain equilibrium in conditions of expanded reproduction. This requires observation of all those proportions between the elements of the matrix, which do not violate the conditions of the internal symmetry between the rows and columns of the matrix.[61] Exactly this symmetry is a condition of economic harmony and sustainable development of economy, toward which the market economy always tends. But, because of the spontaneity of market relations, it achieves it only by chance and cannot stay long in it.

---

[61] This process is easily modeled in Excel.

CONCLUSION

1. To understand the functioning of a market economy dialectical analysis of economic phenomena and processes is required. As a result of this study economics appears as operationally closed complex nonlinear system of economic actions, which have a number of properties that have been well studied in synergetics, constructivism and second-order cybernetics. This allows drawing the unique scientific developments of these disciplines for the study of economic processes in the form of interdisciplinary analysis. Sociology has long used with great success structurally functional approach for the analysis of social systems, to which economic system also refers. Analysis of the economy as a social system in the context of "meta-theory" of T. Parsons and N. Luhmann clarifies many issues of economic theory. In this regard, of particular importance are many ideas of T. Parsons, relative to the system of social actions, and N. Luhmann, regarding the operational closeness and causal openness, autopoiesis and self-reference of social systems, etc. As a result, of interdisciplinary analysis of decentralized economic system we get an entirely new interpretation of economic categories and relationships between them, a new understanding of economic equilibrium, cyclical fluctuations and other processes.

2. In contrast to the natural sciences, in social sciences, theories are able to change the way of system's operation. Economic reality is formed by collective actions. But collective actions depend on the knowledge gained from the cognition of economic reality. When physicists have changed their ideology from classical Newtonian mechanics to modern quantum mechanics, the behavior of the atom has not changed. But theories developed by A. Smith, K. Marx, J. M Keynes, M. Friedman and others have changed the behavior of economic systems.

3. The main contradiction that drives economic system is that each subject consumes that another produces, and produces what consumes another consume, therefore, wants to buy what the other has, and, to sell what the other wants. That is, the satisfaction of own needs is mediated by the satisfaction of others' needs. Because of this by their actions all subjects are attached to each other and form a single whole, a system in which the law of symmetry is fulfilled - all that is produced is consumed, and all that is consumed - is produced.

Moreover, each of economic actors simultaneously is a producer and consumer, seller and buyer, investor and consumer in debt, entrepreneur and saver, creditor and debtor. It is impossible to be a producer of goods, not being a consumer of others' goods, and it is impossible to be a consumer, not being a producer, and it is impossible to be neither one nor the other, without being the seller of own goods and the buyer of others' goods, and it is impossible to be neither seller nor the buyer of goods not being the buyer and seller of money.

In such conditions, each economic action generates another action. That is, there arise the recursive processes, thanks to which the economic system becomes a closed self-reproducing system and is likened to a living organism, which itself generates the cells of which it consists. Such self- reproducing systems are called autopoietic systems, which are studied in the framework of second order cybernetics and constructivism.

> "Autopoiesis is a notion that requires systemic closure. That means organizational, but not necessarily thermodynamic, closure. Autopoietic systems are thermodynamically open, but organizationally closed. Without going into details I would like to mention that the concept of closure has recently become very popular in mathematics by calling upon a highly developed branch of it, namely, Recursive Function Theory. One of its concerns is with operations that iteratively operate on their outcomes, that is, they are operationally closed. Some of these results are directly associated with notions of self-organization, stable, unstable, multiple and dynamic equilibria … " (Foerster, 2003, 281).

4. For adequate understanding of reproduction process of the economy as of a complex self-organizing system, it is necessary to clearly recognize the difference between "causal openness" and "operational closeness" of the system. Under the causal openness is meant the principle underlying the interchange of matter, energy and information of economic system with its environment, whether it's the nature, human body or culture. But under the functional, operational or organizational closeness is meant the principle

forming the immanent structure of economic system and providing the self-organization processes of decentralized economy. The given model just tries to simulate the organizational closeness of economic system, and thereby, to reveal the difference between the purely technological and purely economic aspects of real economic processes. Functional closeness is caused by interconnection of all economic functions (production, consumption, demand, supply, investment, consumption in debt, thrift, entrepreneurship, etc.) in a single system, and form a closed structure. Only thanks to this it becomes possible to understand the reproductive process as a circular process in which, from a purely economic point of view, the results of economic activity at the same time are its preconditions. That is an economic system appears as autopoietic system, as a system, which itself creates the elements of which it is composed (like a living organism). In this approach, the production and consumption of intermediate products are the processes occurring only inside the production sector and are intended for internal consumption.

5. The property of self-organization leads the economic system to a state of equilibrium. In a market economy there is a counter directed movement of commodity and money flows, which form a closed loop. These counter flows balance each other and form a single system, to which the symmetry property is inherent. The state of equilibrium is the state of symmetry. Self-organization implies the restoration of inner harmony and symmetry of economic system in which the integrity of economic system is restored. In this state all the elements of system are necessary parts of the whole. Here all proportions precisely follow; there are no deficits and no surpluses.

6. The symmetry literally permeates the entire world around us.[62] The concept of “symmetry” is generally used in two senses. In one sense, symmetrical means something proportional; symmetry shows that way of harmonizing of many parts with which they are united into a whole. The second meaning of the word is - balance. The economic system manifests the symmetry property in both these senses. Various economic flows are mutually agreed upon; they complement and balance each other, forming a single unit

[62] Still in the beginning of the 20th century, Academician V. Vernadsky wrote that the new in science was not the revealing of symmetry principle, but revealing its universality. The development of science increasingly confirms this truth. Indeed, the totality of symmetry is striking. Fundamental phenomena studied by cosmology, physics, chemistry, biology, social and other sciences, in one form or another show signs of symmetry. The symmetry underlies in the theory of relativity, quantum mechanics, solid state physics, atomic and nuclear physics, elementary particle physics. The realization of that the symmetry as well as the asymmetry accompanying it, inherent in the economy as well as in the rest of nature, allows for a deeper grasp of the economic laws (See: Leiashvily, 2011).

as a self-regulating system with "feedback." The famous German mathematician, physicist and philosopher Hermann Weyl wrote in his "Symmetry": "state of equilibrium must be apparently symmetrical" (Weil, 1968, 55). It follows that the equilibrium model that adequately reflects the economic processes must have the symmetry property.

7. The market economy is a complex nonlinear dynamic operationally closed system in which self-organization is carried out thanks to a recursive processes – commodities are produced by commodities, prices are formed by prices, actions are generated by actions, needs generate new needs, etc. Such recursive processes in the economic system as well as in other complex nonlinear dynamical systems generate "Eigen values," " Eigen behavior," "Eigen functions," "Eigen algorithms." Just such "Eigen values" are the equilibrium prices and the equilibrium quantities of goods, the "Eigen behavior" are fluctuations in economic activity according to "Eigen algorithm."

Like many other complex systems a market economy is both operationally closed and causally open. Accordingly, it simultaneously strives for balance within the system (between the intra-system processes) and is in a non-equilibrium state with respect to the environment. That is, it possesses an inner equilibrium and stability, which is necessary to preserve the integrity of the system and possesses the external imbalance and instability in relation to the external environment, which is a necessary condition for the development of the system. Therefore, it is able to homeostasis and, at the same time, is able to develop, modify state, respond to external influences and adapt to the environment, that is, is capable of dynamic equilibrium.

8. The "symmetric model" is an attractor, i.e. it is relatively stable, latent structure, to which inevitably yield the processes of development in a market economy, as to causally open non-linear system. Nonlinear mathematical models of complex systems show that such systems "hide" a certain form of organization of intra-processes, which are caused solely by their own non-linear properties. That is, these structures – attractors can be interpreted as a teleological structure, which determines the main evolution tendencies of the system. The idea of "attractor" in chaos theory resembles the concept of the essence in dialectics and the ideas of ancient thinkers about the potential and non-manifested. In particular, it is conformable with Plato's notion about some of the first-samples and perfect forms in the world of ideas, to which the things of visible, always imperfect world tend to be like. Or to the notion of Aristotle on the entelechy, about some internal energy, inherent in matter, and forces it to find certain form.

9. That, what the given model reflects, isn't visible behind external manifestations of relationships between private subjects with their conflicting interests. In the article considers the movement of counter-directed commodity and financial flows, which form the closed contour. These flows, caused by objective economic laws, form "live" self-developing and self-regulated system. Though finally it is brought to motion by energy of egoistical interests of millions independent private subjects, but, nevertheless, this system doesn't depend on a will of separate subjects. On the contrary, it structures this energy of egoism and forces private subjects to act in one way or another by causing their economic decisions. Just this system of interdependent economic flows generates that anonymous force, which binds them into a single economic organism and makes them dependent from each other, though they do not quite realize logic of this interdependence and think that they operate only in their own interests. This anonymous force and system of economic flows are outcome of market mechanism and division of labor due to which subjective egoism turns to assistance to satisfaction of all others (See: Hegel, 1990, 240).

10. The given model just reflects formation logic of concrete parameters of resource allocation into various products' manufacturing and imputation of products to resources (to production factors). At that level of abstraction, on which the model is constructed, only that is important in conditions of production factors' scarcity that their services should be paid by corresponding quantity of products, but it is not important whether the subject pays for factors' services belonging to other subjects, or pays a payment to himself for services of his own factors. It is as though only "legal" side of problem.

In real economy not only various consumers own simultaneously various production factors and their services, but also various producers manufacture simultaneously various kinds of products. Until monopolies arise, for functioning of decentralized economic system it is not important how production factors (and incomes from them) are distributed between millions of private owners or how manufactures of various goods (and incomes from them) are distributed between millions of private entrepreneurs. This distribution can be most different. So, from positions of this model it is important what shares of products to various production factors are amputated, but not how this production factors (together with products manufactured by them) between private subjects are distributed.

11. The "Symmetric model" shows the "necessary" macroeconomic proportions between the volume of production and consumption of goods produced by various departments (i.e. groups of branches) of economy. Macroeconomic equilibrium is not disturbed as long as these proportions are

respected. But within each of departments the relatively small deviations from equilibrium in some branches are compensated by opposite deviations - in others. Such deviations are not reflected on the macrolevel, demonstrating the range of stability of macroeconomic equilibrium toward the microeconomic imbalances. "Necessary" proportions of reproduction assume that at the macroeconomic level in economy is produced only what is consumed and is consumed only what is produced.

In a market economy the real proportions of reproduction constantly fluctuate relative to the "necessary" proportions. Behind these fluctuations of market economy it is difficult to see the "necessary" macroeconomic proportions, which provide full harmony and consistency of economic processes. Nevertheless, these "necessary" proportions exist. They are caused by objective laws. At that they are necessary not only for the market, but also for any economic system. Although the mechanisms to maintain these proportions are different in natural, market and regulated economy. If economic policies would be able to ensure the preservation of these proportions between departments of economy, the economy will be able to completely get rid of cyclical fluctuations and to achieve sustainable growth.

12. In the focus of neoclassical theory is the process of production, but not of reproduction. Reproduction is infinitely renewable, continuous production process. This means that as a result of such production its ***premises***, the conditions for continuing production are also reproduced. Therefore, without an understanding of this process it is impossible to explain functioning of economy as integrity, as a living organism.

One of the main conditions, without which production cannot continue, is reproduction of economic subject itself. This already means that it is important to analyze not only production of products, but also their consumption. For consumption of products is reproduction of economic subject and, together with it, is reproduction of economic needs and incentives, which drive the entire economy. It is also important that in the ***"consumption of final products***" the theory can recognize the ***"reproduction of primary resources,"*** reproduction of property rights and other necessary conditions of production. For in a market economy, the primary resources are the rights to use the services of production factors, which exist as goods and only owners of production factors can sell them. The reproduction of primary resources in a market economy is reduced to the reproduction of property rights on production factors, therefore, to reproduction of subjects of property.

13. But the reason of misunderstanding of significant interdependencies among the most important financial flows lies in the methodology of scientific

analysis. Namely, the economic paradigm does not consider the deep inner connection between production and consumption in general. But consumption and production are the opposite moments of the same process of economic activity. They are inextricably linked. Production of products is consumption of resources and consumption of products is the reproduction of resources. For primary resources are services of production factors. At that, in conditions of commodity production these resources exist as a specific commodity – as the right of temporary use of production factors' services sold by owners of these factors. Therefore, reproduction of primary resources is reduced to reproduction of life of owners of production factors, and hence reduced to consumption of final products by these owners.

It turns out that production of products is the consumption of resources, and consumption of products is reproduction of resources. The sector of production of final products is the sector of consumption of primary resources and the sector of consumption of final products is the sector of reproduction of primary resources. Each of these sectors produces goods that are consumed by the opposite sector. Therefore, production and consumption sectors are inextricably linked to each other through the exchange of products and resources. Just because of this they are necessary to each other, are necessary parts of a whole. This whole just dictates the proportions of social production, consumption, distribution and exchange. This whole is a market economy "producing commodities by means of commodities" (P. Sraffa).

14. The gross profit and gross saving are also intrinsically linked. From the viewpoint of reproduction, as a permanently renewable process, profit is the same surplus of incomes over expenditures for current consumption in production sector, as saving is - in consumption sector. Profit is the "saving" of producers and saving is the "profit" of consumers, and they both occur during production and consumption of commodities in conditions of one and the same price system. After all the alternation of incomes and expenditures takes place in both spheres of production and of consumption. Producers' incomes are consumers' expenditures and producers' expenditures are consumers' incomes. Accordingly, the difference between incomes and expenditures takes for them the mirror opposite forms - profits and saving. That's why the profits and saving are intrinsically linked. As soon as the incomes of ones are expenditures for others and vice versa, the profits and saving cannot be independent variables. Since the incomes and expenditures of both producers and consumers depend on the prices of products and resources, the greater the products' prices are ahead of the resources prices, the more are profits and the less are saving; and vice versa. The more resources' prices rise

and products' prices reduce, the greater are the saving and the lower are the profits. That is, in a market economy the ratio between the prices of primary resources and finished products in the opposite way is reflected on the amount of gross profit and gross saving. Both of them is a leak from the circulation of "incomes and expenditures" of consumers and producers. But for maintaining a balance in circulation it is necessary that income leakage from each of these two sectors should be offset by inflows of invested funds from the opposite sector. Macroeconomic equilibrium condition is the equality of gross profit and gross saving that are fully invested in physical, human, natural and public capitals.

15. Income and saving are only money equivalent of surplus product and saved resource. In reality, depreciation and net growth of all types of capital are made by surplus product and surplus resource. In the process of economic reproduction, in addition to the necessary products and resources, surplus products are reproduced in production sector, and in consumption sector - surplus (saved) resources. However, these sectors do not exchange them on each other like a necessary product and resources. They invest them into each other. This means that each of these sectors not only provides its goods to other sector for consumption in debt, but also itself consumes in debt the goods from the opposite sector. Hence, it is clear that the economic equilibrium implies equality of such economic flows, as profits, saving, investment and consumption in debt.

Investment and consumption in debt are the opposite moments of one and the same process. For example, investment of primary resources in production of physical capital is the consumption of these resources in debt, but in the sphere of consumption, the consumption in debt of final products is investment in human capital, etc. If society consumes in debt more than invests in production of capital, it means that it ineffectively uses the stocks of resources and products. Ultimately, this means that the investment is made not through abstaining from current needs, but through the restricting of future needs. That is, the burden of investment is shifted to future. But when the future becomes the present, it would appear that either production capacities are reduced or the rate of their growth reduces. The consequence of this is the slowing growth or recession in all economy.

16. By the inability to know the essence of economic processes the fact is caused that the neo-classical theory, though fixes the relationship between saving and investment, is not aware of relationship between saving and profit as well, between investment and consumption in debt. So, it does not realize connections between all of the above mentioned categories (profit, saving,

investment and consumption in debt), which exist within a closed economic system. But without this it is impossible to understand how reproduction is performed, how a general equilibrium is formed and how economic cycles arise. Consequently, without an understanding of these processes it is impossible to create an adequate mathematical model of a decentralized economic system and develop an effective economic policy (See: Leiashvily, 2011, 2012).

According to neoclassical theory an artificial stimulation of consumer demand allows avoiding the depression. But in doing so, it only postpones depression over time, by this future depression inevitably increases. This policy does not allow the market mechanism to dispose of disproportions in economy. Result is an implicit accumulation of internal disproportions. But sooner or later, they appear as a deep and prolonged crisis, during which just happens a restoration of damaged proportions happens.[63]

17. The economic expansion and recession are the self-stimulation and self-locking of economic processes within the turning points - the peak and bottom. Expansion of production promotes the increases of incomes, and increasing of incomes promotes expansion of production. At a recession everything is the opposite. Reducing of production leads to a reduction of incomes and the reduction of incomes leads to reducing of production. Expansion and recession nourish themselves with each new turn reinforcing itself up until they reach these extreme points. Production growth helps to reduce the relative prices on products and their growth on resources. Decline in production, on the contrary, promotes the growth of relative prices on products and reduce them on resources. When the divergence between gross profit and gross saving reaches its culmination, then there occurs a change of propensity to produce and the propensity to consume. That is, the change in the ratio of relative prices of products and resources in the points of phase change of economic cycle causes the change of propensities to produce and consume. The phase of the economic cycle is changed and the process continues on the principle of self-excitation or self-locking until a new turning point will be reached. The market's self-regulation is caused by the very nature of market relations. The economic agents independently make decisions

[63] Something similar happened in the world economy, which just provoked a global economic crisis of 2008. Unrestrained growth of consumption in debt in the last decades in developed countries has led to a violation of proportions between economic flows - profit, saving, investment and consumption in debt. In this sense we can say that the blame for the global crisis of 2008 should be assigned to the neoclassical theory, which has long served as the conceptual basis for policies of demand stimulation.

and nobody knows in advance what total resources the society has, what the total needs of society are, where the maximum of its production capacity is, where the minimum of its consumption possibilities is, and still more do not know where the "point of optimal functioning" of economy is.

In such conditions the market self-regulation of society's economic activity cannot be done differently than the fluctuations between the extreme points of peak and bottom. Like a pendulum a market economy is moving by inertia from one extreme to another, but it cannot stop at the point of equilibrium. Thus, the periodic downturns in economic activity are due to the economic cycle, having an endogenous nature.

However, crises can arise also as a result of a specific reaction of economic system on purely external factors, such as natural disasters, social catastrophes, bad economic policies, and others. This specificity for reaction is caused by an intrinsic nature of the market economy as a complex nonlinear system. If under the influence of these factors deviations of the economy from the equilibrium state will bring it beyond the stability threshold, the crisis may develop in another "scenario." Such crises have already entirely exogenous nature and are no longer the next phase of endogenous economic cycle. To such crises should be attributed the world's major economic and financial crises in 1857, 1873, 1907, 1914, 1929-1933, 1957, 1973-1974, 1987, 2008 - 2010. Such crises are no longer a deviation from equilibrium state, but they themselves are the new equilibrium state under conditions of deep recession. In contrast to the equilibrium at full employment, the equilibrium in a recession is stable; overcoming these crises can be difficult and time-consuming.

18. According to SNA the value of final product is formed on the basis of value added principle. This means that the indicator DP should not include a value of worn-out capital, because "the concept of added value should exclude charges for consumption of fixed capital. ... Last is the newly created value" (SNA 2008, 34). On the other hand, during the year the capital goods were produced, by which worn out capital was replaced. If their value is additionally introduced into the indicator DP, it turns out that the value of National Product is greater than of National Income and besides it contains the value of depreciated capital. Accordingly, there arises a discrepancy between the amount of incomes generated during production of final product and the value of that final product, which must be purchased in the markets by these incomes. It turns out that aggregate supply is greater than aggregate demand; therefore, there are inevitable crises, etc. It is clear there are some unresolved theoretical problems. Despite this, division of indicators DP and NI in the

"gross" and "net" takes place both in neoclassical theory and in all versions of SNA (including the SNA 2008).

19. Smith has got round this problem by introducing the concepts of "gross" and "net" national products. From a theoretical point of view it's a mistake. A. Smith has spread out on incomes the capital expenditures inside the values of separate products in order to avoid a double counting. By this, within the national product and national income, he has not ignored the expenditures of consumed capital, but has only expressed them in a different form. This is fully justified from a scientific point of view. But then, not understanding fully the logic of reproductive process, he has spread out the mentioned indicators on the "gross" and "net." That is, to the mentioned figures, called by him as "net" and calculated through using a value added method he has once again added the value of consumed capital, receiving "gross" figures. But by this, he has once again brought into the "gross" indicators the double counting, which he has wanted to get rid of. Today many articles are devoted to shortcomings of GDP, but not enough attention is paid to its main fault, the fact that it contains a double counting and is logically incompatible with the principle of value added. That is, from a purely theoretical viewpoint GDP as a measure of final product of society is nonsense.

20. The value of produced capital goods, replacing depreciated capital, is contained both in DP and in NI. But it is contained in different forms. In DP, it is contained in the form of depreciation allowances included in the value of final products. At the same time, the capital goods are not in composition of DP, which replace the worn capital, because they do not apply to the final products and are not intended for the final consumption. In NI, on the contrary, it is included in the form of incomes generated during the production of capital goods replacing depreciated capital. At that, in composition of NI a depreciation fund is not included, because it is not a primary income. And since the incomes, generated during the production of capital for replacing the depreciated capital, eventually are formed just from the depreciation fund, the values of DP and NI are equal. All this is due to the fact that there has been an exchange of capital goods, replacing depreciated capital, on the part of surplus product of other branches relevant to their depreciation allowances. Thus, both Domestic Product and National Income, each according to its nature and without violating the value added principle, reflect the value of capital goods produced for replacement of depreciated capital.

21. SNA is based on this or that understanding of reproduction process. But the conceptual basis of the 2008 SNA (as well as all previous versions) is

a neoclassical theory, which does not adequately understand the reproduction process. Therefore, the 2008 SNA gives a distorted view of real parameters of economic processes. The very division of the main macroeconomic indicators of GDP, NDP, GNI and NNI to "gross" and "net" is fundamentally wrong. It follows that classification and formation methods of many other indicators of the SNA also require appropriate adjustments.

22. Economic science has long been considered more advanced than other social sciences and put by them as example. As a result, neoclassical economists have formed professional arrogance of superiority that prevents them from being more susceptible to the scientific achievements of other sciences. Talcott Parsons has believed that economic science is more advanced than sociology and therefore sociology must accept from there the ideas valuable for it. He has tried to do this and has created the theory of social actions with synthesized achievements of systems theory of those days, economic theories of A. Marshall and V. Pareto. His disciple Niklas Luhmann, on the basis of system approach, has proposed a theory of social systems, significantly enriched with new ideas, also perceived from the achievements of related sciences of his days. Thanks to these scientists and their followers, systematic approach in sociology has been widely recognized and has made a huge contribution to the development of sociology. Today, when economic science is clearly in deep crisis, it is high time it should "learn" from sociologists. It should not only accept from them the valuable scientific ideas, but the very willingness to accept the achievements of other disciplines.

The current economic crisis has shown that neoclassical theory and the equilibrium models based on it cannot help in solving the real economic problems. Suddenly it has become clear to everyone that these models are out of touch with reality. Mark Blaug writes: "'Economics for economics' sake will soon become, indeed already is, the battle-cry. At this point, someone might observe that economics is too important a subject to be left to economists." Under such circumstances the task of scientists is to radically rethink the neoclassical paradigm and "breathe life" into the lifeless model of economic equilibrium.

Appendix A

Table 2. Economic flows in a closed economy

Sector 1		Sector 2	
C_p Costs of production	P_n profit	GDP	NDP
I_g – gross investments into production (consumption on credit of recourses) 1. depreciation 2. net increment in physical capital 3. changes of stocks of product	P_I - profit in production of investment goods	I = S **I** – inflow in production sector **S** – outflow from the consumption sector	
GNI	P = D **P** – outflow from the production sector **D** – inflow in consumption sector	S_I - saving from the profits of entrepreneurs (depreciation charge)	**D_g** - consumption of products in debt (gross investment in consumption sector) 1. consumption of entrepreneurs 2. net investments in human capital 3. stock changes of products
NNI		S_n saving	C_c Costs of consumption
Sector 3		Sector 4	

Appendix B

Table 3."Symmetric model" taking into account the intermediate production

The market of intermediate products — Production of intermediate products

$x'_m p'_m$	...			$-P'_m$	$-a'_{m1} x'_m V'_1$	$-a'_{m2} x'_m V'_2$	...	$-a'_{m(n-1)} x'_m V'_{(n-1)}$		
...	...	...	...	...	...	...	...	...		
	...	$x'_2 p'_2$		$-P'_2$	$-a'_{21} x'_2 V'_1$	$-a'_{22} x'_2 V'_2$	..	$-a'_{2(n-1)} x'_2 V'_{(n-1)}$		
	...		$x'_1 p'_1$	$-P'_1$	$-a'_{11} x'_1 V'_1$	$-a'_{12} x'_1 V'_2$	..	$-a'_{1(n-1)} x'_1 V'_{(n-1)}$		
$-P'_m + \sum a' x' v'$	...	$-P'_2 + \sum a' x' v'$	$-P'_1 - \sum a' x' v'$	-	$-a_{11} x_1 V_1$	$-a_{12} x_1 V_2$	...	$-a_{1(n-1)} x_1 V_{(n-1)}$	$-P_1$	
$-P'_m + \sum a' x' v'$	...	$-P'_2 + \sum a' x' v'$	$-P'_1 - \sum a' x' v'$	-	$-a_{21} x_2 V_1$	$-a_{22} x_2 V_2$	...	$-a_{2(n-1)} x_2 V_{(n-1)}$	$-P_2$	
...	...	...	...	-	...	...	..	...	...	
$-P'_m + \sum a' x' v'$	...	$-P'_2 + \sum a' x' v'$	$-P'_1 - \sum a' x' v'$	-	$-a_{(m-1)1} x_{(m-1)} V_1$	$-a_{(m-1)2} x_{(m-1)} V_2$	..	$-a_{(m-1)(n-1)} x_{(m-1)} V_{(n-1)}$	$-P_{(m-1)}$	
					$-a_{m1} x_m V_1$	$-a_{m2} x_m V_2$	...	$-a_{m(n-1)} x_m V_{(n-1)}$	$-P_m$	$x_n p_m$
									$y_n v_n$	
								$y_{(n-1)} V_{(n-1)}$		
							...			
						$y_2 v_2$				
					$y_1 v_1$					

Consumption of intermediate products

Table 4. "Symmetric model" taking into account the export/import

$-a_{11}x_1v_1$	$-a_{12}x_1v_2$	...	$-\alpha_1 A_1$				x_1p_1
$-a_{21}x_2v_1$	$-a_{22}x_2v_2$	...	$-\alpha_2 A_2$			x_2p_2	
...	...	...	...		...		
$-a_{m1}x_mv_1$	$-a_{m2}x_mv_2$	...	$-\alpha_mA_m$ $-P'$	x_mp_m $I = S$			
			$P = Q$ y_nv_n	$-S'$ $-\beta_nB_n$	...	$-b_{n2}p_2y_n$	$-b_{n1}p_1y_n$
		....		...	...	...	...
	y_2v_2			$-\beta_2B_2$	...	$-b_{22}y_2p_2$	$-b_{21}y_2p_1$
y_1v_1				$-\beta_1B_1$	...	$-b_{12}y_1p_2$	$-b_{11}y_1p_1$

REFERENCES

Crutchfield, J.P., J.D. Farmer, N.H. Packard, and R.S Shaw (1986). Chaos. //"*Scientific American."* Vol. 255, No. 6, pp. 46-57.

Foerster H. (2003). Understanding Understanding: essays on cybernetics and cognition. Springer-Verlag New York, Inc.

Fukuyama F. (2005). The End of History and the Last Man. Moscow. "AST: Ermak" (In Russian).

Haken G. (2003). The Secrets of Nature. Synergetics: the doctrine of interaction. - Moscow-Izhevsk: Institute of Computer Sciences (In Russian).

Hawken, P., Lovins, A., Lovins H. (1999). Natural Capitalism: Creating the Next Industrial Revolution Little, Brown and Company.

Hegel G. (1990). Philosophy of Right. Moscow. Misl. (In Russian).

Hegel G. (1974). Encyclopedia of the Philosophical Sciences, volume 1. Moscow. Misl. (In Russian).

Hicks J. R. (1949). 'Mr. Harrod's dynamic theory,' Economica, 16(62): 106–21.

History of Economic Thought. (2002). / Ed. B. Avtonomova, O. Ananina, N. Makasheyuy. Moscow. INFRA-M. (In Russian).

Hudson M. (2010). "From Marx to Goldman Sachs: The Fictions of Fictitious Capital, and the Financalization of Industry." (2010). Critique. A journal of socialist theory, Vol. 38, No. 3, August, pp. 419- 444.

Kalecki, M. (1968). 'The Marxian equations of reproduction and modern economics', in J. Osiatynski (ed.) *Collected Works of Michal Kalecki,* (eds) V*ol. II, Capitalist Economic Dynamics*, Clarendon, Oxford, 1991, pp. 459-466.

Karlin S. (1964). *Mathematical Methods and Theory in Games, Programming, and Economics.* Moscow. Mir. (In Russian).

Keen S. (2011). Debunking Economics: The Naked Emperor Dethroned? London & New York, Zed Books Ltd.

Keynes, J. (1977). The General Theory of Employment, Interest and Money. Moscow. Progress. (In Russian).

Kirdina S. (2011). Institutional change and the Curie principle // Economics of Contemporary Russia. 2011. №1 (52) S.8-19.

Kniazeva E., S. Kurdyumov. The synergetic paradigm. Basic concepts in the context of cultural history. (http://lib.icr.su/node/1247)

Leiashvily P. (2013). Economics in the Grip of Empiricism and Dogmatism. Tbilisi. SIAHLE. (In Russian).

Leiashvily P. (2012). Economic Activity: Teleological Analysis. NY, Nova Science Publishers.

Leiashvily P. (2011). Economic Activity: Teleological Analysis. Tbilisi, SIAHLE. (In Russian).

Leiashvily P. (2011). "The Dialectics of Economic Activity (In Searching of Symmetry in Economy)," *Georgian International Journal of Science and Technology*, V.3, Issue 3.

Leiashvily P. (1996). "Towards the teleological understanding of economic value." // *International Journal of Social Economics.* Vol. 23, N 9. (p. 4 - 14).

Luhmann N. (2007). Introduction to Systems Theory. Moscow, Logos. (In Russian).

Luhmann N. (2007a). Social Systems. Essay on the General Theory. St. Petersburg, Science. (In Russian).

Luhmann N. (2004). Society as a Social System. Moscow, "Logos," (In Russian).

Luxemburg, R. (1968). *The Accumulation of Capital*. New York and London: Modern Reader Paperbacks.

Marx, K. (1992). Capital, Volume II. Penguin Classics.

Marx, K. (1978). Capital. Critique of Political Economy. V.1. Moscow, Politizdat. (In Russian).

Marx K. and Engels F., (1958). Works. V.12. Ed. 2nd. Moscow, Politizdat. (In Russian).

Meteliov A. (2011). Chaos Theory in the Bank. Omsk: Publishing House of the Omsk Institute (branch) RGTEU. (In Russian).

Mises L. (1996). Human Action. A Treatise on Economics, Fourth Revised Addition, Fox & Wilkes, Sun Francisco,

Morishima M. (1991). General Equilibrium Theory in Twenty-First Century.// *The Economic Journal*, V.101, № 404 (January): 69-74.

Moseley, F. (1998). 'Marx's reproduction schemes and Smith's dogma'. In Arthur, C.J. and Reuten, G. (eds), *The Circulation of Capital: Essays on Volume Two of Marx's Capital*, Macmillan, Basingstoke, pp. 159-186.

Parsons T. (1949). The Structure of Social Action. Glencoe. Illinois. The Free Press.

Pluschevskaya U. (2012). On consistency of theoretical foundation of inflation targeting and neo-Keynesian general equilibrium models. // *"Voprosi ekonomiki,"* 2012, № 5, p. 22 - 36. (In Russian).

Prigogine I., Stengers I. (1986). Order out of Chaos: Man's New Dialogue with Nature. Moscow. Progress. (In Russian).

Shultz, T. (1971). Investment in Human Capital. N.Y., London.

Smith, A. (1977). An Inquiry into the Nature and Causes of the Wealth of Nations. Moscow. Sotsecgiz. (In Russian).

Solow R. (2010). "Building a Science of Economics for the Real World." House Committee on Science and Technology Subcommittee on Investigations and Oversight.

Sraffa P. (1999). Production of Commodities by Means of Commodities. Moscow. UNITY. (In Russian).

Steadman, I. (1981). 'Ricardo, Marx, Sraffa.' in Steadman, I., Sweezy, P. & others, *The Value Controversy*, London, Verso Editions and NLB, pp. 11-19.

Stiglitz, J., Sen, A., Fitoussi, J.P. (2009). Report by the Commission on the Measurement of Economic Performance and Social Progress. (www. stiglitz-sen-fitoussi.fr)

System of National Accounts 2008. (2009). European Commission, International Monetary Fund, Organization for Economic Co-operation and Development, United Nations and World Bank, New York.

Toporowski J. (2002). The End of Finance: Capital Market Inflation, Financial Derivatives and Pension Fund Capitalism. Routledge.

Trigg A. (2006). Marxian Reproduction Schema. Routledge.

Walras L. (2000). Elements of Pure Economics. Moscow. Izograf. (In Russian).

INDEX

A

abstinence, 16, 20, 35, 38
actions, vii, viii, xi, xv, xvi, 1, 3, 4, 5, 6, 7, 8, 9, 59, 60, 65, 66, 67, 68, 69, 70, 71, 74, 80, 82, 83, 84, 85, 101, 102, 104
actor, 1, 5, 6, 65
agents, xvi, 26, 31, 35, 36, 68, 80, 82, 91, 98, 109
aggregate demand, 76, 90, 110
aggregate supply, 90, 110
Alexander, 3
allocation, 54, 55, 81, 92, 105
Aristotle, 104
Arrow, xvi, 42, 43, 44, 57, 77
Arrow-Debreu model, 44, 57
Ashby, 1
assets, 21, 23, 25, 27, 39, 52, 53, 90, 96
asymmetry, 103
attractor, viii, 42, 46, 85, 104
autopoiesis system, 3
average market prices, 58
average rate, 36, 37

B

balance, 21, 37, 38, 40, 57, 60, 68, 75, 86, 103, 104, 108
banks, 27
barter, 27, 58
behavior, 2, 41, 42, 73, 75, 78, 79, 81, 82, 83, 84, 85, 101, 104
benefit, 50, 61, 86
Beytson, 1
Blaug, 43, 112
blind spot, 87
Bortkiewicz, xvii
budget, 17, 22, 48
burden of entrepreneurial risk, 38
business cycles, ix, xi, xiii, 28, 53, 74
businesses, 5
buy, vii, 12, 13, 15, 17, 23, 24, 31, 47, 48, 49, 56, 67, 80, 102
buyer, 7, 8, 13, 17, 47, 102

C

Capital, 12, 13, 17, 18, 48, 49, 95, 116, 117, 118
capital goods, 17, 18, 20, 22, 23, 26, 35, 89, 92, 98, 99, 110, 111
causality, xvi, 2, 59, 63, 66
causally open system, viii, xiii
cause, 2, 36, 40, 42, 50, 58, 59, 63, 64, 73, 75, 76, 77, 82, 96
chaos theory, vii, xi, xiii, xvi, 41, 65, 104
charge, 21
choice, 6, 24, 60, 81
circular causality, xv, 1, 59, 63, 64, 82
circular flows, xvii

circularity, 41, 44, 45
circulation, 27, 38, 39, 108
closeness, viii, 9, 29, 31, 58, 63, 65, 69, 103
Coase, 43, 81
cognition, xv, 1, 70, 74, 101, 116
commodity, 13, 32, 37, 39, 43, 45, 48, 49, 68, 76, 82, 89, 103, 105, 107
communication, 5, 20, 21
complex system, ix, xi, 3, 4, 10, 57, 69, 73, 74, 75, 76, 77, 79, 83, 84, 104
consider, xvi, 5, 38, 60, 74, 91, 107
constructivism, vii, xi, xiii, xvi, 1, 2, 3, 29, 40, 101, 102
consumption, viii, ix, 7, 8, 9, 11, 12, 13, 14, 15, 16, 18, 19, 20, 21, 22, 23, 24, 25, 26, 27, 28, 31, 32, 33, 34, 35, 37, 38, 39, 40, 45, 47, 48, 49, 51, 52, 53, 55, 56, 57, 58, 59, 60, 64, 68, 82, 90, 91, 92, 94, 95, 96, 97, 98, 103, 105, 106, 107, 108, 109, 110, 111
consumption goods, 90
consumption in debt, ix, 9, 19, 22, 23, 24, 25, 26, 27, 28, 34, 37, 38, 48, 52, 55, 68, 98, 103, 108, 109
consumption of products, 95, 106, 107
consumption process, 18
consumption sector, 11, 12, 14, 15, 18, 20, 23, 39, 51, 52, 92, 94, 97, 98, 107, 108
cooperation, 67, 75, 86
cost, 20, 21, 24, 25, 32, 38, 46, 48, 49, 52, 57, 81, 89, 95, 98
credit, 7, 9, 17, 26, 27, 37, 48, 52, 53, 56
crisis, xv, xvii, 1, 21, 73, 76, 77, 80, 81, 83, 84, 85, 86, 109, 110, 112
cybernetics, vii, xi, xiii, xvi, 1, 2, 3, 29, 40, 63, 73, 101, 102, 116
cycle, xvii, 38, 39, 40, 58, 59, 73, 75, 76, 109, 110

D

debt, ix, 7, 8, 9, 19, 20, 25, 26, 27, 28, 37, 47, 60, 67, 96, 98, 102, 108, 109
debtor, 7, 8, 102
decentralized economic system, vii, ix, xi, xvi, xvii, 4, 10, 29, 42, 76, 101, 105, 109
decentralized economy, viii, 3, 43, 45, 46, 58, 93, 103
decision, 25, 26, 80
demand, viii, 8, 9, 32, 37, 38, 39, 45, 47, 51, 53, 56, 57, 58, 68, 90, 99, 103, 109
department, 92, 96, 97, 99
depreciated capital, 19, 20, 52, 89, 97, 98, 110, 111
depreciation, 18, 19, 20, 21, 22, 23, 24, 35, 52, 92, 95, 96, 98, 99, 108, 111
depression, 76, 85, 86, 109
deviation, 40, 46, 76, 79, 87, 110
deviations, xvii, 57, 91, 106, 110
dialectical analysis, vii, ix, xi, xiii, xviii, 3, 40, 42, 101
dialectical contradiction, 12
dialectical relationships, 10, 64
distribution, 14, 24, 28, 32, 49, 53, 81, 82, 91, 94, 105, 107
division of labor, 7, 9, 91, 105
Domestic Product, 92, 98, 111
DP, 92, 98, 99, 110, 111
durable, 18, 19
dynamic equilibrium, viii, 60, 61, 75, 76, 83, 85, 91, 104
dynamic systems, 57, 77

E

economic activity, viii, 19, 28, 39, 61, 74, 75, 76, 80, 81, 82, 84, 85, 87, 103, 104, 107, 110
economic equilibrium, vii, viii, xi, xiii, xvii, 29, 38, 44, 45, 60, 68, 73, 84, 86, 91, 101, 108, 112
economic flows, 3, 28, 31, 39, 59, 60, 68, 83, 84, 85, 91, 93, 94, 95, 103, 105, 108, 109
economic subjects, xv, 3, 16, 21, 39, 68
economic system, vii, viii, ix, xi, xiii, 9, 29, 31, 32, 33, 40, 42, 43, 53, 57, 59, 63, 69, 70, 71, 74, 75, 76, 77, 81, 82, 83, 84, 85, 86, 91, 101, 102, 103, 104, 106, 109, 110

economic theory, xi, xvi, xvii, xviii, 3, 29, 42, 84, 90, 98, 101
economy, vii, xi, xiii, xv, xvii, 3, 5, 6, 11, 12, 14, 15, 16, 18, 21, 27, 28, 39, 40, 42, 43, 44, 49, 50, 58, 60, 61, 68, 69, 71, 73, 74, 75, 76, 77, 80, 81, 82, 83, 86, 91, 92, 99, 101, 102, 103, 105, 106, 108, 109, 110, 113
Eigen-Algorithms, 2
Eigen-Behaviors, 2
Eigen-Functions, 2
Eigen-Values, 2
elementary action, 5
employment, 77, 83, 84, 110
entrepreneurial risk, 15, 25, 35, 51
entrepreneurial services, 12, 24, 51, 95, 96
entrepreneurs, 12, 14, 17, 19, 22, 24, 25, 26, 38, 47, 48, 49, 51, 52, 60, 67, 96, 97, 105
Entrepreneurship, 20
entropy, 63, 81, 84
epistemology, 1, 4
exchange, 13, 14, 15, 23, 27, 28, 37, 43, 45, 50, 58, 67, 74, 81, 91, 99, 107, 108, 111
exchange ratios, 15, 45, 58
existence theorem, 44, 77
exogenous crises, 74
expansion, 39, 70, 75, 82, 83, 84, 86, 109
external factors, ix, 45, 46, 67, 68, 73, 74, 75, 76, 77, 83, 110

F

feedback, 4, 40, 76, 104
final products, 13, 14, 15, 16, 17, 19, 20, 24, 25, 31, 37, 45, 47, 48, 49, 56, 91, 92, 94, 97, 98, 106, 107, 108, 111
fluctuations, vii, xvii, 38, 39, 40, 42, 53, 56, 58, 68, 73, 74, 76, 77, 80, 85, 86, 87, 101, 104, 106, 110
Foerster, 1, 2, 4, 40, 41, 42, 46, 59, 63, 64, 65, 66, 102, 116
Fukuyama, 81, 116
functionalism, 3, 4

G

GDP, xiii, xviii, 80, 90, 98, 111, 112
Glasersfeld, 2
goods, 8, 11, 13, 14, 15, 18, 19, 20, 21, 23, 25, 26, 27, 28, 31, 32, 33, 34, 35, 36, 37, 38, 41, 44, 45, 48, 49, 50, 52, 56, 57, 58, 67, 68, 80, 89, 91, 95, 96, 97, 98, 99, 102, 104, 105, 106, 107, 108, 111
government, iv, xv, 5, 17, 21, 22, 24, 40, 48, 52, 74, 87, 97
Great Depression, 76, 85
gross profit, ix, 22, 23, 24, 37, 38, 48, 53, 54, 55, 56, 68, 92, 98, 107, 109
gross saving, ix, 22, 23, 24, 37, 53, 54, 55, 56, 68, 107, 109

H

Haken, 4, 82, 83, 84, 116
Hawken, 22, 116
Hegel, 10, 105, 116
Heilbroner, 44, 45
Hicks, 77, 116
Hudson, 27, 116
human capital, 19, 20, 21, 24, 25, 32, 37, 47, 52, 60, 81, 94, 95, 97, 108

I

incomes, 12, 15, 16, 17, 18, 21, 22, 23, 24, 25, 26, 32, 37, 39, 46, 47, 48, 50, 51, 53, 56, 59, 89, 92, 96, 97, 98, 105, 107, 109, 110, 111
instability, viii, 75, 77, 104
integrity, viii, 4, 31, 48, 58, 65, 68, 70, 76, 82, 83, 91, 103, 104, 106
interaction, 1, 2, 44, 57, 59, 68, 75, 87, 116
interdisciplinary analysis, vii, xiii, 29, 101
interdisciplinary research, 1
interests, xvii, 3, 4, 49, 59, 68, 71, 74, 85, 86, 87, 91, 105
intra-system processes, viii, 45, 104

investment, viii, ix, 9, 17, 19, 20, 21, 22, 23, 25, 26, 27, 28, 32, 34, 35, 37, 38, 47, 48, 51, 53, 54, 55, 94, 98, 103, 108, 109
Iron law, 48

K

Kaldor, xvi
Kalecki, 90, 116
Keynes, xv, 26, 39, 101, 117

L

Labor, 12, 18, 48, 49, 95
Land, 12, 18, 48, 49, 95
Leiashvily, iii, xiii, 7, 8, 13, 16, 24, 26, 27, 91, 103, 109, 117
Leontief, xvii
Lorentz, 4
losses, 38, 57, 61, 80, 85, 86
Luhmann, vii, 2, 3, 5, 63, 65, 69, 101, 112, 117

M

macroeconomic, xiii, xvii, xviii, 28, 50, 67, 91, 105, 106, 112
macroeconomic equilibrium, 28, 50, 91, 106
macroeconomic indicators, xiii, xviii, 112
macroeconomic proportions, 105, 106
Mandelbrot, 4
market economy, vii, viii, xi, xiii, xvi, 3, 7, 8, 9, 10, 11, 12, 14, 23, 27, 28, 29, 31, 42, 48, 58, 59, 60, 61, 67, 71, 73, 74, 75, 83, 91, 99, 101, 103, 104, 106, 107, 108, 110
Marshall, 112
Marx, xvii, 5, 11, 12, 14, 26, 28, 64, 80, 90, 101, 116, 117, 118
mathematical model, viii, ix, xi, xvi, xvii, 29, 42, 78, 79, 104, 109
matrix, 32, 65, 91, 93, 94, 95, 96, 97, 99
Maturana, 1, 2, 4, 63
Merton, 3
Mises, 6, 118
model, viii, ix, xiii, xvi, xvii, xviii, 9, 10, 29, 31, 32, 35, 37, 38, 40, 41, 43, 44, 45, 47, 48, 49, 50, 52, 56, 57, 68, 71, 78, 79, 81, 86, 92, 103, 104, 105, 112
monetary resources, 17, 23, 39, 53
monetary veil, 23, 58
money, 8, 9, 13, 16, 17, 19, 20, 23, 26, 27, 32, 35, 37, 38, 39, 47, 48, 50, 53, 56, 59, 60, 67, 68, 76, 80, 81, 102, 103, 108
money assets, 23, 53
money capital, 26, 27
Morishima, xvi, xvii, 118
Moseley, 90, 118
Munch, 3

N

National Income, 92, 98, 110, 111
natural capital, 18, 19, 21, 22
NDP, 90, 98, 112
necessary product, 15, 16, 17, 46, 47, 108
necessary resources, 16, 91
needs, vii, viii, xv, xvii, 7, 15, 16, 18, 19, 32, 44, 47, 50, 51, 58, 59, 64, 67, 77, 86, 91, 102, 104, 106, 108, 110
neoclassical paradigm, 43, 112
neoclassical theory, ix, xv, xvi, 10, 50, 106, 109, 111, 112
NI, 92, 97, 98, 99, 110, 111
NNI, 112
nondurable goods, 18, 19, 22, 23
nonlinear system, xi, xvi, 3, 73, 74, 75, 80, 101, 110

O

operational closeness, vii, viii, xiii, 9, 45, 63, 65, 66, 69, 101, 102
organizational closeness, viii, 10, 11, 102
organizations, 5
overproduction, 57, 84

owners, 12, 13, 15, 17, 19, 20, 21, 22, 24, 25, 38, 47, 48, 49, 51, 68, 97, 105, 106, 107

P

Pareto, 60, 86, 112
Pareto optimality, 60, 86
Parsons, vii, 3, 5, 101, 112, 118
payment, 15, 17, 19, 21, 22, 24, 38, 46, 47, 50, 51, 53, 58, 60, 97, 105
phenomenology, 3
physical capital, 19, 20, 21, 37, 47, 52, 108
Piaget, 1
Plato, 104
potential, 52, 56, 60, 61, 76, 81, 83, 84, 85, 104
prices, viii, 15, 16, 21, 24, 32, 37, 38, 39, 40, 41, 43, 44, 45, 47, 49, 50, 51, 57, 58, 59, 68, 76, 89, 104, 107, 109
pricing mechanism, 57, 58
Prigogine, 4, 85, 118
primary resources, 12, 13, 14, 15, 16, 17, 19, 24, 25, 31, 35, 37, 45, 47, 48, 49, 61, 91, 92, 94, 95, 96, 106, 107, 108
product market, 17, 37, 38, 48, 56
production, viii, 7, 8, 9, 11, 12, 13, 14, 15, 16, 17, 18, 19, 21, 22, 23, 25, 26, 27, 28, 31, 32, 33, 34, 35, 37, 38, 39, 40, 43, 44, 45, 46, 47, 48, 49, 50, 51, 52, 53, 55, 56, 57, 58, 59, 64, 73, 76, 80, 81, 82, 89, 90, 91, 92, 94, 95, 96, 97, 98, 103, 105, 106, 107, 108, 109, 110, 111, 114
production cost, 32, 51
production factors, 12, 13, 14, 15, 16, 18, 35, 45, 48, 49, 50, 80, 92, 95, 96, 105, 106, 107
production sector, 12, 14, 15, 19, 23, 39, 52, 92, 96, 97, 103, 107, 108
products, iv, 7, 12, 14, 15, 16, 17, 18, 21, 22, 23, 24, 26, 31, 32, 37, 38, 39, 40, 45, 46, 47, 48, 49, 50, 51, 52, 56, 57, 58, 60, 64, 80, 89, 90, 91, 92, 95, 96, 97, 98, 99, 103, 105, 106, 107, 108, 109, 111
profits, ix, 9, 15, 17, 23, 24, 26, 27, 35, 37, 38, 39, 44, 47, 48, 49, 50, 52, 92, 107, 108
public capital, 18, 21, 22, 23, 26, 54, 94, 108

Q

Quesnay, xvii

R

recession, 39, 75, 76, 82, 83, 84, 108, 109, 110
recursive processes, vii, viii, xi, xiii, 2, 29, 36, 65, 102, 104
redistribution, 28, 39, 53, 60, 61, 74, 86, 97, 98
rent, 12, 15, 17, 47, 89
reproducible goods, 12
reproduction, vii, ix, xi, xiii, xvii, xviii, 9, 12, 13, 14, 15, 16, 17, 18, 19, 20, 21, 22, 23, 24, 25, 28, 33, 47, 48, 49, 51, 52, 90, 91, 92, 94, 95, 96, 97, 98, 99, 102, 106, 107, 108, 109, 111, 116, 118
reproduction of resources, 14, 18, 51, 107
resources, 7, 12, 14, 15, 16, 17, 22, 23, 26, 27, 28, 31, 32, 33, 34, 35, 37, 38, 39, 45, 47, 48, 49, 50, 51, 52, 53, 56, 57, 60, 61, 76, 77, 80, 81, 84, 91, 92, 95, 105, 106, 107, 108, 109
resources prices, 107
Ricardo, xvii, 118
rights, iv, 12, 13, 49, 81, 106

S

Samuelson, xvii
saver, 7, 8, 25, 26, 35, 102
saving, ix, 9, 15, 16, 17, 20, 21, 23, 25, 26, 27, 28, 34, 35, 36, 37, 38, 39, 45, 47, 48, 49, 50, 51, 52, 53, 56, 60, 94, 107, 108, 109
Schumpeter, xvii

self-referential system, 2, 57, 69
Shultz, 20, 118
Smith, v, xvii, xviii, 4, 25, 57, 83, 89, 90, 101, 111, 118
SNA 2008, 90, 97, 110
social action, vii, xi, 4, 5, 66, 101, 112
society, xvii, 3, 4, 5, 9, 21, 27, 28, 50, 51, 52, 59, 64, 69, 70, 71, 74, 77, 80, 81, 83, 86, 89, 96, 97, 98, 108, 110, 111
sociology, 2, 3, 63, 65, 75, 112
Solow, xvii, 118
Spencer-Brown, 1
spending, 14, 23, 25
Sraffa, xv, xvii, 12, 15, 31, 49, 107, 118
stability, viii, 4, 77, 83, 85, 104, 106, 110
Steadman, 15, 118
structural functionalism, 3
structural-functional paradigm, 4
subjects, vii, xv, 4, 5, 7, 12, 19, 20, 21, 23, 26, 28, 44, 48, 59, 60, 67, 68, 70, 71, 74, 80, 82, 84, 85, 86, 102, 105, 106
subsystem, 5, 9, 64
surplus products, 16, 17, 22, 23, 26, 27, 47, 92, 99, 108
surplus resource, 16, 17, 22, 23, 27, 47, 48, 52, 53, 108
surplus value, 16, 17, 35, 47
sustainable growth, 106
Symmetric model, xiii, 40, 41, 42, 44, 49, 50, 67, 70, 76, 81, 83, 86, 105, 114, 115
symmetry, 68, 86, 96, 99, 102, 103
synergetic, 29, 117
system, iv, vii, viii, ix, xi, xiii, xvii, 2, 3, 4, 5, 6, 8, 9, 27, 28, 31, 37, 39, 40, 41, 42, 44, 45, 46, 50, 51, 53, 56, 57, 58, 59, 60, 63, 64, 65, 66, 67, 68, 69, 70, 73, 74, 75, 76, 77, 78, 79, 80, 82, 83, 84, 85, 86, 97, 101, 102, 103, 104, 105, 107, 112
System of National Accounts, xiii, xviii, 90, 118

T

taxes, 17, 21, 22, 48, 92
theory of imputation, 48
Toporowski, 27, 118
transformation, 4, 12, 15, 16, 23, 26, 27, 37, 80, 81, 92
Trigg, 90, 118

U

underproduction, 84
utility, 14, 24, 32, 38, 56, 57

V

value, xvii, 13, 15, 16, 17, 20, 24, 28, 32, 33, 35, 41, 42, 46, 47, 48, 51, 67, 68, 69, 80, 86, 89, 90, 92, 96, 97, 98, 110, 111, 117
Varela, 1, 2, 4, 63
variables, 24, 41, 78, 82, 107
velocity of money circulation, 53
Vernadsky, 103
vicious circle, xvi, 57, 59

W

Walras, xvii, xviii, 18, 77, 118
Walrasian model, 49
Weyl, 104
Wiener, 1